DATE DUE

Julius Caesar
and Ancient Rome
in World History

Titles *in World History*

JULIUS CAESAR
and Ancient Rome
in World History

James Barter

Enslow Publishers, Inc.

40 Industrial Road   PO Box 38
Box 398   Aldershot
Berkeley Heights, NJ 07922   Hants GU12 6BP
USA   UK

http://www.enslow.com

C 1   2003   18.85

Library of Congress Cataloging-in-Publication Data

Barter, James, 1946–
    Julius Caesar and Ancient Rome in world history / James Barter.
        p. cm. — (In world history)
Includes bibliographical references and index.
ISBN 0-7660-1461-4
1. Caesar, Julius—Juvenile literature. 2. Heads of state—Rome—
Biography—Juvenile literature. 3. Generals—Rome—Biography—Juvenile
literature. 4. Rome—History—Republic, 265–30 B.C.—Juvenile literature.
[1. Caesar, Julius. 2. Heads of state. 3. Generals. 4. Rome—History—
Republic, 265–30 B.C.] I. Title. II. Series.
    DG261 .B37   2001
    937'.05'092—dc21
                                                        00-012070

Printed in the United States of America

10 9 8 7 6 5 4 3 2 1

To Our Readers: We have done our best to make sure all Internet addresses in this
book were active and appropriate when we went to press. However, the author
and the publisher have no control over and assume no liability for the material
available on those Internet sites or on other Web sites they may link to. Any
comments or suggestions can be sent by e-mail to comments@enslow.com or to
the address on the back cover.

Illustration Credits: © Corel Corporation, pp. 33, 77; Enslow
Publishers, Inc., pp. 6, 14, 16, 21, 26, 65, 106, 109; James Barter, pp. 37,
55; J. G. Heck, *The Complete Encyclopedia of Illustration* (New York:
Park Lane, 1979), p. 10; J. G. Heck, ed., *Heck's Pictorial Archive of
Military Science, Geography and History* (New York: Dover Publications,
Inc., 1994), pp. 62, 90; Library of Congress, pp. 49, 85, 114.

Cover Illustration: © Digital Vision Ltd. (Background Map); Library of
Congress (Caesar Portrait).

Contents

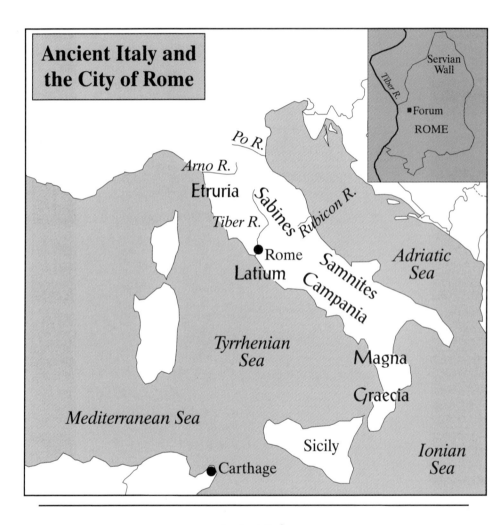

Ancient Italy.

Chapter 1

The Die Is Cast

Great leaders sometimes seize on geography to shape the history of their times. Rivers, mountains, lakes, and oceans have all played major historical roles. The Carthaginian General Hannibal and his army swept across the rugged terrain of the Alps to invade Italy in 218 B.C. The American General George Washington crossed the icy Delaware River to launch a surprise attack on the British on Christmas night, 1776. One hundred years later, the American Indians inspired by Sitting Bull and led by Crazy Horse lured the 7th Cavalry under the command of Lieutenant Colonel George Custer into a ravine where thousands of hidden Indian warriors slaughtered every one of them. So, too, in January 49 B.C., the Roman General Julius Caesar sat in the saddle of his charger, staring across the Rubicon River. As Caesar gazed to the south, he was contemplating his fate and the fate of Rome if he were to cross this river with his army.

The Rubicon River meanders through the low-lying fertile fields of northeastern Italy as it makes its way to the Adriatic Sea. Not quite thirty miles long and barely one hundred yards wide at any point, it is one of dozens of small rivers that irrigate the fertile farms of this region. Although it was not one of the powerful rivers of the world, its location had a special significance for the ancient Romans. It was the boundary that separated Caesar's province of Cisalpine Gaul (made up of modern-day Switzerland and northern Italy) from central Italy. Roman law strictly forbade a governor such as Caesar to cross province boundaries with his army. To do so was punishable by death.

After waging war for nine years in Gaul, Caesar had won an impressive string of spectacular military victories. Defeating one Gaulic tribe after another, he had earned a favorable reputation among his soldiers and many citizens of Rome for his skill and daring. Success on the battlefield often led to success in politics in Rome. For this reason, Caesar's political enemies were becoming very nervous about his victories. To stop his rise to power, they stripped him of much of his authority and called him to Rome. He was told that his term as governor of Cisalpine Gaul had expired, and that he had to return to campaign for reelection. Caesar knew that this was merely a trick to separate him from his soldiers, who would protect him from harm if necessary.

The dilemma that Caesar contemplated as he stared across the Rubicon was whether he should cross alone or with his army. If he crossed alone, his political rival Gnaeus Pompey, along with Caesar's enemies in the Roman Senate, would almost certainly kill him. If, on the other hand, he chose to cross with his army—the 13th Legion, consisting of five thousand battle-hardened soldiers—and then march to Rome, the Senate would declare him an enemy of the state. As such, he would be opposed in ferocious battle by the superior military strength of Pompey, who had been appointed by the Senate to destroy him. At the age of fifty-one, Caesar had much to consider.

Caesar's thoughts that winter day may have focused on several recent events in Rome that had brought him to this dilemma. Rome's success in expanding its far-flung empire had recently changed the social and political climate. As Rome's armies fanned out across most of Western Europe, North Africa, and the Middle East, expanding Rome's territory and wealth, Roman politicians failed to adapt to the many changes that went along with their success.

As the aristocratic ruling class became wealthier, it refused to share its good fortune with the working classes that occupied the lower rungs of the army, the economy, and the government. The small farmers, who gave their services to the Roman Army in times of war, were especially vocal. They demanded more land and money in exchange for their lost limbs and scarred bodies.

Common people, who joined the ranks of the Roman Army in the hope of increasing their wealth and status, were often disappointed. Most returned home just as poor as they had been earlier.

Social unrest flared, pitting small farmers and the urban poor against the wealthy. Street fights broke out in Rome for the first time ever, causing the deaths of many people who had sought a greater share of Rome's wealth and more access to the government. Two brothers who tried to pass legislation to aid the soldier-farmers, Tiberius and Gaius Gracchus, were murdered by powerful aristocrats, along with thousands of their followers in 133 B.C. and 121 B.C., respectively. Mob violence like this had never before occurred in Rome.

Julius Caesar may also have reflected on the fact that his soldiers, who had fought alongside him for nine years, were willing to cross the Rubicon with him. They knew that such an act would throw them into battle against other Roman legions, and they were ready to take that chance. Soldiers' willingness to follow their generals even in defiance of Roman law was a growing problem that never would have occurred in earlier years.

Soldiers had recently begun to show greater allegiance to their generals than to the Roman Senate. Their generals rewarded them for service with land and money that the Senate would not give them. As a result, generals often became more powerful than the elected members of the Senate. This flaw had caused severe and costly clashes between powerful military leaders that had crippled the traditional power of the Senate and the Roman political system. In 82 B.C., when Julius Caesar was a teenager, he witnessed a bloody clash between General Cornelius Sulla and the highest ranking politician in Rome, Gaius Marius. Sulla victoriously entered Rome with his army and butchered thousands of his political enemies, yet did nothing to help the poor of Rome.

Now, as Caesar sat on his horse staring across the river, he also reflected on his rival Pompey, with whom he had once enjoyed a close business relationship and personal friendship. Each man had great respect for the abilities of the other, but their destinies had brought them into different political alliances. In all of Rome, they were the two most powerful and influential men of the time. As aristocrats, soldiers, politicians, and diplomats, the similarities of their lives far outweighed the differences. In fact, their personal lives had once intertwined with the marriage of Caesar's daughter, Julia, to Pompey.

Caesar recognized that the recent violence was caused by the aristocratic politicians in Rome, who had become more focused on their personal needs than on the well-being of Rome. Caesar himself was often guilty of this same shortsightedness. However, Caesar, unlike Pompey, was willing to discuss helping the poor farmers who had valiantly fought for generations in the Roman legions.

Caesar spurred his horse on and splashed across the Rubicon at the head of his legion. As he did so, he uttered his now famous words, *"iacta alea est"*—Latin for "the die is cast." Caesar had rolled the dice of fate. His decision to cross the river could not be changed. With this act, Caesar set in motion events that could never be reversed. By the time Caesar had reached the far side of the Rubicon, the war was on.

Within five years, battlefields would be soaked in Roman blood, the Mediterranean Sea would be littered with the wreckage of fleets, and the Roman Republic would begin to fall. Professor Erich Gruen at the University of California in Berkeley considered Caesar's defiant crossing of the Rubicon River the single most significant event in the history of Rome.[1]

Chapter 2

Rome at the Crossroads

The 1,229-year span of Roman history, from 753 B.C. to A.D. 476, witnessed the dramatic rise and fall of Rome's fortunes. Battle-tested legions fanned out across the face of Europe, the Middle East, and North Africa, subduing all who dared to oppose them. In time, every inch of land touched by the warm Mediterranean waters lay within Rome's grip, as did the cold, mountainous lands to the north.

Rome's fortunes soared and plummeted for more than a millennium, largely because of the quality of its leadership. During Rome's twelve centuries of greatness, dozens of capable leaders stepped forward to flex their political muscle, trying their luck at ruling the most dominant, unpredictable, and fabled civilization of its time. The changing nature of Roman politics never encouraged the selection of the best-qualified

Before the period of Rome's expansion, several civilizations shared influence on the Italian peninsula.

candidates for leadership. Politicians were usually selected from a relatively small number of wealthy privileged families or by reckless force of arms. By the time Rome had plunged beyond the point of no return in A.D. 476, a relatively small number of politicians had managed to rule effectively, while a large number of inept men had faltered at the post. This plunge, made famous by the eighteenth-century English historian Edward Gibbon's great work, *The History of the Decline and Fall of the Roman Empire*, was not the first such fall. The first, that of the Roman Republic, had taken place five hundred years earlier.

Ruling the Early Republic

The great names of Roman history are not scattered evenly along its lengthy timeline. Like other major civilizations, Rome sometimes experienced periods of decline because of mediocre leadership. Other periods of ascent saw a surplus of highly effective leaders. The period of the Republic was one such remarkable time. Beginning in 509 B.C. and ending 482 years later in 27 B.C., the Republic had an unusually high number of outstanding leaders.

The Rome into which Julius Caesar was born in 100 B.C. was experiencing dramatic changes. Rome at this time was enjoying the riches of military conquests that extended from Spain in the west, Greece and parts of the eastern Mediterranean to the east, Egypt and North Africa in the south, and France and parts of Germany in the north. In spite of Rome's huge empire, the Rome of Julius Caesar was going through a monumental breakdown.

At the beginning of the Republic in 509 B.C., Rome's leading politicians did not have the time or experience to establish a formal, written constitution. Instead, they ruled the new Republic by borrowing many of the old traditions and political institutions from the kings who had ruled from 753 to 509 B.C. Although the laws of the early Republic were unwritten and were based on the institutions of the kings, they did not establish another dictatorship.

An Experiment With Democracy

When the last king was expelled in 509 B.C. by families who were tired of being excluded from politics, the

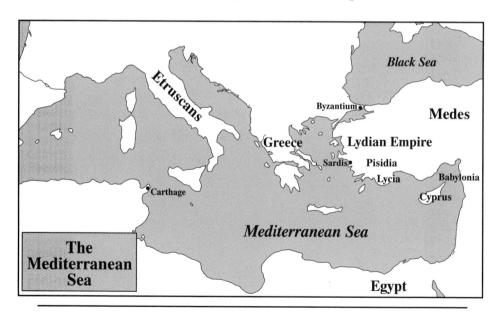

The Mediterranean Sea and the cultures surrounding it, as they looked around 600 B.C.

Republic was started as a bold experiment. The new leaders hoped to create a form of government that would prevent the return of the dictatorship they had detested under the kings. This new form of government was an early form of democracy. Many historians today credit the Greeks in Athens with being the first to conceive the idea of democracy. In fact, the Athenians and Romans were developing their respective democracies independently at roughly the same period in time.

Source Document

The consuls, when in Rome prior to leading out their armies, are in charge of all public affairs. For all of the other public officials with the exception of the tribunes, are below the consuls and subject to their authority. . . . The Senate, first of all, has control of the treasury, for it has complete authority over all revenues and expenditures. For the quaestors are unable to disburse funds for any particular need without a decree from the Senate. . . .[1]

Ancient historian Polybius described the powers given to the different parts of Roman government in this account of the Roman Republic's constitution.

Replacing the king as the highest elected officer were two leaders called consuls. To avoid having any semblance of dictatorial power, the two consuls were elected for only a one-year term. Each held veto power over the other, which meant mutual agreement was required on all decisions. Only members of select elite families qualified for the consulship. These privileged families were few in number. Their high status came from their ancestry and wealth, not skill or experience. During the Republic, most of the consuls came from only a handful of these families. This created what historians call an *oligarchy*—meaning rule by a small number of people. During the one-hundred-year period between 233 and 133 B.C., 50 percent of the consuls came from only ten of these privileged families, while 80 percent came from twenty-six of them. When the consuls left office after their one-year term, many continued their political careers in the Senate.

The purpose of the original Senate during the period of the kings was to advise the king. During the early Republic, the Senate took a strong role in foreign policy, matters of finance, and state religion. The three hundred members of the Senate were chosen from the old aristocratic families and ex-officeholders and served in the Senate for life.

During the Republic, tradition, not written laws, specified the rules for the election of the senators and their constitutional power. Real political power during the Republic was primarily focused in the hands of the patrician families—those with special connections to other influential families. Some, but not all, patrician families ruled because of wealth. Some ruled because of long-standing family ties with other families. Besides the consuls, the aristocrats also dominated the lesser offices such as the *quaestors*, who managed the treasury; the *praetors*, who functioned as judges; and the *censors*, who controlled access to citizenship.

In 494 B.C., within twenty years after the founding of the Republic, a few wealthy nonaristocratic families called the plebeians came to believe that the new democracy should be expanded to include them as well. A few plebeian families began to agitate to have some of their representatives elected to office. The plebeians finally gained the right to elect ten tribunes from their group to represent their interests. The plebeians then declared that these tribunes could veto many decisions of Roman magistrates, or officials, and could veto any decision or legislation by the Senate. The plebeians had also won for themselves the right to author their own legislation.

The ten tribunes were elected annually. Their function was to protect the well-being of the plebeians. Since they had the power to veto the acts of the consuls, they served as the leaders of the plebeians in their struggles with the patricians.

To further the evolution of the democracy, in 367 B.C., the Licinian-Sextian laws provided that one of the two consuls had to come from the ranks of the plebeians. This ended the patrician monopoly controlling the consulship.

An Experiment With Imperialism

While the experiment with democracy was taking hold in Rome, a second experiment with imperialism began to take center stage. Rome's fame as one of the first superpowers began with humble beginnings along the banks of the Tiber River.

The early Romans recognized that the Tiber was the lifeline of the city. Born close to its banks, the city grew up and expanded slowly along the river, taking advantage of its many benefits. Throughout Roman history, the Tiber served as a source of food, a place of recreation, a means of transportation, a path to the sea for sewage disposal, and a natural line of defense.

Early Rome occupied about three square miles that included the fabled Seven Hills of Rome. By the end of the period of the kings, Rome had expanded only modestly beyond the Tiber, either by diplomacy or force, to include a few neighboring tribes.

The Italian Wars

During the early years of the Republic, Rome's newly discovered sense of imperialism led the Romans to begin to flex their military muscle. They sought to overwhelm three formidable civilizations beyond Rome: the Etruscans of central Italy, the Volscians southeast of Rome, and the Aequians east of Rome. Conquering these cultures after ten years of warfare that ended with the ten-year siege of the Etruscan city of Veii in 396 B.C., Rome took control over central Italy.

Following a short period of peace, Rome turned its gaze toward the Samnites, who lived in southern Italy. After a series of three wars beginning in 343 B.C. and ending in 290 B.C., Rome defeated the Samnites. Flushed with the excitement of victory, Rome then moved against the Greek colonies of southern Italy. After wars that lasted another fourteen years, Rome

This map shows the territories on and around the Italian peninsula that were taken over by Rome in the years up to 218 B.C.

21

completed the conquest of southern Italy by defeating the Greek King Pyrrhus in 275 B.C. Rome now controlled the entire Italian peninsula from the toe as far north as the Arno and Rubicon rivers and the Apennine Mountains.

All the lands and peoples Rome had conquered failed to satisfy it. Eleven years after defeating Pyrrhus, Roman politicians rekindled their aggression. They now wished to add the island of Sicily to their territory. It seemed only natural to the Romans that Sicily, separated from the Italian peninsula by nothing but the narrow Strait of Messina, should belong to them.

Seizing Sicily would be much more challenging than other Roman conquests had been. Carthage, a major trading and military power directly across the Mediterranean on the North African coast, occupied the island. Founded in the ninth century B.C. by Phoenicians who lived on the eastern Mediterranean Sea, Carthage had controlled all of the western Mediterranean with little opposition until Rome began expanding. The Romans called the Carthaginians *Punici*, the Latin word for Phoenicians, which is translated to *Punics* in English.

Reckless hunger for the island of Sicily would nearly cost Rome its entire empire. Most Roman historians regard these imperialistic wars as the most dramatic of Rome's long history. Clashing with Carthage in three separate wars that spanned 118 years, Rome planted the seeds of the Republic's later destruction.

The First Punic War

The First Punic War broke out in 264 B.C. It began because of a dispute over the city of Messana on the island of Sicily. This was a risky war for the Romans because all their previous military conquests had been land wars. They had no experience with naval warfare.

With the aid of Greek ship builders, the Romans began to build a fleet by copying Carthaginian warships. Rome's first great sea battle was fought in 260 B.C. It allowed Rome to seize the cities of Agrigentum and Mylae. Following a few setbacks over a period of several years, the Roman Navy finally won a second stunning victory over the Carthaginian fleet in 242 B.C. This loss to the Roman fleet forced the Carthaginians to surrender Sicily to Rome. As demonstrated by their victories over the Carthaginian fleet, the Romans not only mastered naval warfare, but they improved on it.

Up to five hundred men rowed early warships that were fitted with long pointed rams on the bow of the warship, just below the waterline. The ram was similar to a telephone pole with a sharp end that was capped with metal—usually bronze. The objective in early naval warfare was either to smash a hole in the side of an enemy ship with the ram, or to sheer off the oars of the enemy ship, leaving it dead in the water.

Roman sailors had an advantage over the Carthaginians because of an entirely new weapon— the *corvus*, a long wood plank. The corvus was hinged at one end on the deck of a Roman ship and winched into the vertical position by ropes. The end in the air was fitted with a long iron spike. When a Roman ship came close to a Carthaginian ship, the captain dropped the plank, slamming it down on the enemy ship. An instant after the spike hit the enemy ship's deck, Roman soldiers stormed across the corvus and fought the stunned and unsuspecting Carthaginians in hand-to-hand combat.

Rome had accomplished two objectives by war's end: It had successfully continued expanding its territory and had established itself as a major naval power. Carthage, although shaken, had not been crushed. Planning to avenge the defeat, Carthaginian General Hamilcar Barca began planning to take the war to the walls of Rome. To achieve this, he set up a military base of operations south of the Ebro River in Spain. Upon his death in 221 B.C., his son Hannibal assumed control of the invasion. This became the Second Punic War.

The Second Punic War

In 218 B.C., Hannibal crossed the Ebro with a force of about ninety thousand soldiers, twelve thousand cavalry, and thirty-seven elephants. His army pushed northeast across the frozen Alps, then descended into the plains of northern Italy at a cost of close to half his troops.

Just twenty-five years old, Hannibal received the aid of local tribes, who hated the aggressive Romans. Hannibal's objective was to fight all Roman armies on his way to destroy Rome.

A brilliant strategist, Hannibal lured the Roman armies into battles where he was able to outmaneuver them. The first major battle of the Second Punic War took place at Trebia in northern Italy. Hannibal defeated the Romans, killing thirty thousand soldiers. The Romans were so stunned that they withdrew most of their remaining forces.

The next critical battle took place at Lake Trasimene on the morning of June 24, 217 B.C., while a thick layer of fog hugged the lake's shoreline. Most of the twenty-five-thousand-man Roman Army was drawn up on the plains opposite Hannibal's remaining twenty-seven thousand troops. The two huge armies clashed for three hours. After the battle, the Roman Army fled to Rome, leaving behind fifteen thousand soldiers who were cut down along with their commander, Gaius Flaminius.

One year later, near the city of Cannae, Roman consuls led two armies totaling seventy thousand men against Hannibal's army of only forty thousand. As the Romans confidently advanced with most of their strength in the center, Hannibal intentionally allowed them to break through his infantry. Thinking they were winning, the Romans foolishly surged ahead for the kill. Hidden from view, however, to the left and to the right, the Carthaginian cavalry closed in on the advancing Romans in a pincer move. At this point, the remaining Carthaginians counterattacked. Trapped, with nowhere to retreat, the Roman soldiers panicked. The ensuing slaughter was horrific. The next day, when two thousand wounded survivors staggered back to Rome, the population nervously awaited the return of the remainder of the seventy thousand soldiers, only to learn that no more would be coming home. Nearly sixty-eight thousand soldiers lost their lives on that one day. It was the worst defeat any Roman army would ever suffer.

Because the Romans were unable to defeat the Carthaginians, Hannibal was free to range up and

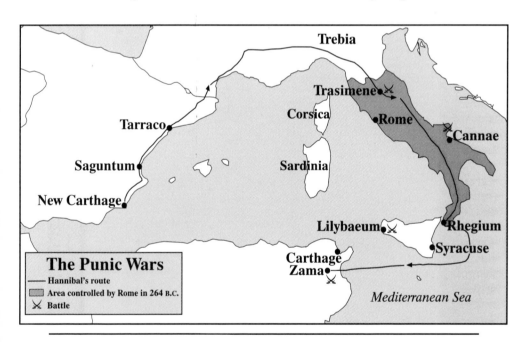

The major battles of the Punic Wars, including the route taken by Hannibal through the Italian peninsula, are seen on this map.

down the central spine of Italy, stealing grain and cattle from local farmers to feed his army. After fifteen years of Hannibal's pillaging the Italian landscape and devastating small farmers, Roman General Publius Cornelius Scipio proposed a new strategy to stop him. To end the death grip that Hannibal held on much of Italy, Scipio decided to divert him by invading Carthage.

When Hannibal learned of Scipio's attack on Carthage, he immediately withdrew from Italy, crossing the Mediterranean to defend his homeland. In 202 B.C., at the town of Zama, Scipio managed to defeat Hannibal and his army. The Carthaginians lost their remaining navy, all of Spain, and an enormous payment in silver and gold. With the close of the Second Punic War, Rome controlled all of the western Mediterranean.

The Third Punic War

The Carthaginians, who for centuries had depended on sea trade, rebuilt their merchant ships and began to flourish again. The Romans, deeply suspicious of Carthage and still stinging from the humiliation of Hannibal's reign of death in Italy, demanded that the Carthaginians abandon their city and move inland into North Africa. When Carthage refused, the Roman Senate, led by the elder statesman Cato, declared war in 149 B.C. This marked the start of the third and final Punic War.

After a three-year siege during which Carthaginian pleas for mercy were ignored, the Romans smashed through the walls of Carthage, burned the city, and slaughtered most citizens, selling the others into slavery. One final act has remained infamous throughout history. The Romans loaded wagons full of salt and spread it over Carthage's dark, fertile farmland to guarantee that the city's lush crops would never again grow. This mass slaughter, followed by the salting of the earth, ranks to this day as one of the most heinous acts of war ever inflicted. In 146 B.C., Carthage ceased to exist.

The Eastern Wars

Rome's appetite for war seemed to have no limit. In the midst of the Punic Wars, Rome turned its well-disciplined army loose on Greece and Macedonia (located along Greece's northern border). In a series of four wars starting in 215 B.C., Rome pounded the Macedonians. By the end of the last war in 148, Rome controlled all of Macedonia and tried to seek a peaceful settlement with the Greeks, whom the Romans greatly admired. Despite Rome's military success, internal squabbling among the Greeks would continue to be a constant problem for the Romans.

The Greeks' inability to organize successfully made them a tempting target for Macedonia, which had invaded Greece in the past. Out of great frustration, Rome recognized that the only solution to the Greek problem would be to invade Greece and rule it as a Roman province. In 146 B.C., a Roman army marched into Corinth, north of the Peloponnesus Peninsula, and destroyed the city. The Romans hoped this would be a sign to the rest of the Greek states that Rome would not tolerate any further rebellions.

Controlling all of the Mediterranean by 146 B.C., the Romans arrogantly called the Mediterranean Sea

Source Document

And how it may be well asked, what part is left to the people in this government: since the Senate, on the one hand, is vested with the sovereign power . . . in all things that concern the management and disposal of the public treasure; and since the consuls, on the other hand, are entrusted with the absolute direction of the preparations that are made for war. . . . There is, however, a part still allotted to the people; and, indeed, the most important part. For, first, the people are the sole dispensers of rewards and punishments; which are the only bands by which states and kingdoms, and, in a word, all human societies, are held together. . . . The people, then, when any such offenses demand such punishment, frequently condemn citizens to the payment of a fine. . . . To the people alone belongs the right to sentence any one to die.[2]

Polybius described the government and society of Rome just after the end of the Punic Wars.

Mare Nostrum, Latin for "Our Sea." No nation now dared to challenge Rome. From the eastern shores of the Mediterranean to the western gates of Gibraltar, Rome had achieved the military and political unity that had eluded other nations and other leaders. The Greek historian Polybius wrote a history of Rome that covered this extraordinary period because, as he said:

> ... who is so worthless or indolent [lazy] as not to wish to know by what means and under what system of polity [government] the Romans in less than fifty-three years have succeeded in subjugating [controlling] nearly the whole inhabited world to their sole government—a thing unique in history?[3]

Chapter 3

Civil Strife and the Late Republic

The final defeat of Carthage, combined with Rome's expansion into Greece and the Middle East, at long last heralded an end to more than six generations of warfare. Rome could not have hoped for a better international position. It now dominated the Mediterranean, to the delight of Roman citizens. However, while these lengthy military conquests had solidified Rome's grip over its empire, they had precisely the opposite effect on its citizens at home.

Hannibal's Legacy

Two profound changes historians consider significant causes of the fall of the Republic were soon to surface in Rome. Both can be traced to Hannibal's fifteen-year occupation of Italy while he ravaged small farms to feed his army. The first change was friction between

Rome's social classes, which surfaced within one generation of the end of the last Punic war. The second change was the disintegration of loyalty toward Rome within the Roman Army. Hannibal could never have guessed that the legacy of his defeat would one day be viewed as one of the major causes of the fall of the Roman Republic generations after his death.

Not all Roman citizens emerged from the hardships of the Punic Wars with their fortunes intact and with high hopes for the future. The fifteen-year destruction of small farms by Hannibal to feed his army during the Second Punic War forced many poor farmers to sell their homes and land. This problem was doubly severe because most loyal Roman soldiers were small farmers who would take up arms in times of war and then return to their farms in times of peace. Besides the destruction of their farms, they now faced the harsh reality that they were paid very little for their soldiering. The Roman Senate did not feel obligated to compensate them fairly for defending their homeland. Life in the army was not yet viewed as a legitimate full-time occupation.

Without their farms to support their families, the destitute small farmers migrated to Rome and other large cities to find humble work. The wealthy, on the other hand, whose fortunes had been safe within Rome's walls during Hannibal's occupation, had grown wealthier from the spoils of the wars. Seeing the plight of the farmers, the wealthy bought the abandoned small farms and combined them to make large

These carvings of Roman soldiers can be found on Trajan's Column in Rome.

estates. From this time on, wealthy landowners would dominate Roman agriculture, while the poor farmer-soldiers would dominate the slums of Rome.

The displaced peasant farmers flooded into Rome and other urban centers. Failing to find jobs, they soon had no place to sleep and little to eat. The problem of finding employment was made worse because of an unusually large influx of slaves from conquered lands. In addition to seizing territory and money as spoils of war, wealthy Romans also acquired tens of thousands of slaves. Roman historian H. H. Scullard explained: "It [slavery] took two forms: while the more barbarian captives would be sent by their Roman masters to work on their lands, the more cultivated Greek slaves were . . . employed as secretaries, teachers, and doctors."[1]

Owners of farms and shops who would normally hire employees now had slaves to work for them. For small farmers who had lost their land, the prospect of finding work was bleak. As this condition worsened, the numbers of homeless people grew. The poor became increasingly desperate and angry. For the first time in the history of Rome, problems among the civilian population became more severe than problems with the foreign populations that Rome controlled and administered.

Friction Between the Social Classes

At the cost of the blood of thousands of peasant Roman soldiers, the prizes of war flowed into Rome from conquered lands. Every imaginable foreign item could be found in marketplaces throughout the city. On a daily basis, seagoing cargo ships rowed by slaves and blown by winds carried the riches of Rome's provinces. They plied the length of the Mediterranean to feed the growing appetite of Rome. These wood freighters carried staples such as grain, dried vegetables, salted meats, building materials, home furnishings, and clothing, as well as luxury items to beautify and enhance the lives of the rich. The wealthy particularly favored Egyptian linen and dyes; Greek marble, wine, and wondrous foods; Lebanese furniture crafted from exotic hardwoods; and Middle Eastern spices and jewelry. Rome during the last century of the Republic had grown fat as the capital of its far-flung provinces and the master of the Mediterranean world.

The kaleidoscopic sights, sounds, and smells of exotic goods unloaded from boats that docked along the wharves on the Tiber River thrilled busy shoppers who eagerly snapped up the latest foods and merchandise. Exciting as these times may have been, there was a dark side to them that would soon fracture Roman society. As is often the case with prosperity, competition for these riches created tension between the wealthy and the poor.

Although a few Roman families enjoyed their wealth in glittering palaces staffed by dozens of servants, most Romans lived in squalid, high-rent, wooden apartments without running water and with barely enough food for their families. Boasting a population of close to one million, the smell of sewage and the clatter of wagon wheels bouncing over cobblestone streets night and day were sources of constant complaints. Rome and other large Italian cities, with populations between twenty thousand and forty thousand, teemed with unskilled laborers and displaced farmers who were subject to the whims of their employers. Under these circumstances, most workers lived in debt, with little prospect of relief. Without laws governing wages and conditions of employment, the future was bleak for most families. Their children could expect little improvement.

Some men could find minor relief by joining the Roman Army. But even this road out of poverty presented the soldiers with special problems and tended to lead them back to the same squalid conditions they had hoped to escape. The soldier's length of service varied over time. The average was sixteen years, but at times it could be as high as twenty-five. The work was physically punishing, and many soldiers were forced to serve far from home along dangerous frontiers. When they were not fighting wars, soldiers sometimes filled their time by building forts and camps. If, by chance, soldiers were still alive at the end of their years of service, the best they could hope for was a small amount of money. Retirement plans and pensions did not yet exist. Common soldiers generally left the army in the same state of poverty they were in when they entered.

Who Ruled Rome?

This uneven distribution of wealth and the resulting strife it created between the social classes was by no means a new reality. The reason for this economic inequality lies in the answer to the question: Who ruled Rome?

Although the Roman Republic was basically a democracy, the wealthy class of patricians had for hundreds of years controlled the elections of the highest offices, such as the consuls and the Senate. When elections were held, there was fierce politicking for the vote, but regardless of who won, the man was almost always from one of the old, elite families. These families

The ruins of the Senate House, where the prominent politicians of the Republic met to make laws for Rome.

often created alliances that split them into rival groups. In this way, these few families would support their own candidates and could successfully exclude any new families from entering their ranks. Enjoying this political monopoly, the wealthy had little motive to help the poor. These few privileged families focused their attention on their own financial and political fortunes, not on those of the common people.

This political inequality began to go through subtle changes not long after the Punic Wars. It was at this time that the Republic began to witness some politicians who were willing to champion the cause of the poor. These politicians worked with the tribunes elected by the common people to pass laws, rather than with the aristocrats who controlled the Senate. Their motive was partly to relieve the poverty of the poor and to create better jobs. But mostly, they hoped to further their own personal success.

It became clear to a few leaders of the nobility that they might be able to advance their own careers by supporting legislation that would attract the votes of the poor citizens who qualified to vote. Qualifications changed over time, but generally only free male citizens could vote. Sometimes land ownership was a voting requirement. At best, probably no more than 10 to 15 percent of the population voted, although this did vary over time. Still, the votes of the poor became important enough to encourage politicians to go out of their way to court the votes of the common people. This novel tactic created a split that divided the wealthy into two political parties: the Optimates and the Populares.

Optimates and Populares

Virtually all citizens in Rome aligned themselves with one of the two political factions: the *Optimates*, meaning "the best people," or the *Populares*, meaning those who considered themselves connected to the common people, or populace. These terms are confusing and can easily be misunderstood. Modern historians disagree over the differences between the two parties.

The leaders of each party generally came from a relatively small number of old established families that had strong connections with each other through marriage. Family ties within each party were very important. Most, but not all, of these families were quite wealthy. Although some modern historians tend to think of the Optimates as representing the interests of the rich and the Populares as representing the interests of the poor, neither ever actually passed much legislation to assist the poor. Although the Populares often spoke of helping the poor, seeking to work with the tribunes in exchange for votes, they actually did very little.

Competition for land and goods between the rich and poor quickly escalated to competition for political power as well. From the days of the early Republic, the noble families had controlled the most important political offices—consuls and Senate—leaving lesser offices to commoners. As commoners, the soldiers who had fought to extend the boundaries of the empire now wanted a greater share in the politics and wealth of Rome. Small farmers who had put down the plows and shovels of their farms to take up the swords and shields of the army wanted more land to farm. They also wanted a more significant role in the politics of Rome as a reward for their sacrifice.

During the later years of the Republic, bands of roving political gangs led by ambitious politicians fought in the streets of Rome. This violent behavior highlighted the growing internal strife between the two groups. The eventual clash between the Optimates and the Populares was caused by greed. As a result of the personal ambitions of a few wealthy and powerful men, all of Rome was dragged into the fray.

First Blood—The Gracchi Brothers

The first blood spilled in the class conflict between the rich and poor flowed from the veins of the tribune Tiberius Sempronius Gracchus (*Gracchus* is the singular form of the name; *Gracchi* is the plural) and his supporters. In 133 B.C., without the approval of the aristocratic leaders of the Senate, Tiberius proposed land reform legislation that would take farms held by the rich and redistribute them to the poor. He believed no one should be allowed to own more than 640 acres of land. Tiberius's attitude was remarkable, considering that the Gracchi family was one of Rome's noble families. His support of the poor made him the first great leader of the Populares.

Angered by his attempt to give land to the poor without the approval of the Senate, a group of wealthy senators representing the Optimates and their followers killed Tiberius and three hundred of his supporters. This act represented the first politically motivated mass murder in Roman history. It would not be the last.

Although Tiberius passed his legislation, much of it was later overturned. Nonetheless, he triumphed in history as the first Roman politician who attempted major political change without the support of the old aristocratic families. His appeal to the general population of voters identified him with the Populares and those who sought to improve the lives of the common citizens—or at least said that they would.

Ten years after Tiberius's death, his brother, Gaius Sempronius Gracchus, won the office of tribune. Following his brother's example, Gaius passed a law to provide cheaper food to the poor of Rome without consulting the Senate. Such legislation reduced the amount of money many wealthy merchants would make. This angered the Optimates. Gaius further angered the Optimates in 121 B.C. when he proposed expanding citizenship to certain Italian tribes allied with Rome without first holding the customary discussion with the Senate. The Senate, furious at Gaius for circumventing its authority, declared him an outlaw and murdered him, along with three thousand of his followers.

Source Document

At last Tiberius Sempronius Gracchus, an eminent man, ambitious for honor, a forceful orator, and for these causes well known to everybody, made an eloquent speech, while tribune . . . deploring that a people so warlike . . . were gradually sinking into pauperism and decreasing in numbers. . . . [H]e once more brought forward the law providing that no one should hold more than five hundred iugera [a measurement of land] of public land. . . . This greatly vexed the wealthy. . . .[2]

This account explains how Tiberius Sempronius Gracchus angered the wealthy citizens of Rome with his ideas for changing the distribution of wealth.

So significant were the unprecedented deeds of these two Gracchi brothers that most modern Roman historians consider their acts the beginning of the fall of the Republic. Some historians point out that blood had flowed through the streets of Rome before the Gracchi brothers made their entry on the scene. These same historians admit, however, that it had never been done with such savagery. Together, the Gracchi brothers made history by breaking ranks with the old aristocratic families and passing legislation without the consent of the Senate. To stop others from following in the Gracchi brothers' footsteps, the Optimates resorted to murdering the brothers and their followers. Even such extreme tactics, however, could not stop the momentum of the Populares.

The shell that had protected the elite aristocratic families for generations from the misery and agitation of the struggling poor had cracked. No amount of political maneuvering could repair the break. The Optimates, however, did not see the crack. There is no evidence to suggest that the problems the Gracchi brothers started caused the Optimates much concern. Although the magnitude of the disturbances was unprecedented, as long as the loyalty of the army was assured, the Optimates believed they could preserve their control over Rome.

Marius and the Army

Roman armies had a long history of uncompromising loyalty to their government. During the long period of Rome's expansion, Roman farmers leaving their families and croplands for faraway battlefields had been a way of life. The Senate had offered these farmer-soldiers very little in the way of pay or retirement. They were expected to serve out of a sense of loyalty, not for profit, although they did receive plunder from vanquished enemies.

There had been a long tradition of this dual lifestyle, but now the demise of the small farmer was creating a stressful situation. The growing dissatisfaction among soldiers was swelling the ranks of Populares. Gradually, the once-loyal army was turning into an instrument of destruction.

Ten years after the murder of Gaius Gracchus and his supporters, the old aristocratic Optimates hoped that the Populares cause had been permanently crushed and that life in Rome could now return to normal. This would not be the case. In 112 B.C., a rebellion in Africa started by King Jugurtha of Numidia—a country south of Carthage—caught the attention of Rome. Following six years of skirmishes without an end to this irritating revolt, Senate leaders began complaining about the inability of the Roman Army to defeat a minor enemy. The army's failure contrasted sharply with the legions that had fought the length and breadth of the Mediterranean years before to make Rome the most feared nation in Europe.

Finally, in 107 B.C., Gaius Marius, a consul, stepped forward. He proposed that he could defeat Jugurtha if he could recruit his own army from the urban poor and landless farmers. His solution to the problem of poor soldier quality and low morale was to promise his soldiers land and money following a successful campaign.

This was a revolutionary change that was every bit as significant as the reforms of the Gracchi brothers. Never before had any leader, other than those in the Senate, made promises of rewards to Roman soldiers. To Marius, this was simply a new tactic he could use to raise an army that was enthusiastic to fight and win a messy war in Africa. To Republican political traditions, however, this would end the long-standing tradition of Senate control over the armies and an equally long-standing tradition of armies loyal to Rome rather than to their individual commanders. The Senate was experiencing another significant loss of authority, as it had following the reforms of the Gracchi brothers.

Marius, unlike all other consuls before him, was not born into one of the old aristocratic families. He was referred to as a *novus homo*, Latin for "new man." This meant he was the first of his family to serve as a consul and in the Senate. As a new man, Marius was sympathetic to the cause of the Gracchi brothers and was a firm advocate of the Populares, as were most Roman soldiers. Marius knew he could recruit good soldiers who would fight successfully against King Jugurtha if he could deliver to them better rewards than the Senate could.

After Marius recruited his own army, the people of Rome sent him and his first lieutenant, Lucius Cornelius Sulla, to end the disturbance in Numidia. A superb strategist, Marius subdued Jugurtha after a series of prolonged skirmishes. As he had promised his troops, Marius allowed them to plunder the defeated Numidians. He also arranged for land and other benefits to be given them on their return to Rome. For the first time in many generations, the soldiers felt they had been fairly paid for their soldiering. For the first time, too, they recognized that their general, Marius,

45

was able to provide them with better rewards than the Senate had ever done.

Just as historians point to the Gracchi brothers as the first sign of a faltering Republic, many point to Marius and his personal army as the second sign that the end was rapidly approaching. This change in the nature of the Roman Army made possible the rise of military dictators, who would now use their loyal armies as instruments to destroy each other. In so doing, they would destroy the Republic as well.

Julius Caesar was one such man. His personality and temperament were suited for this time and place in history. Few politicians in Rome during the last generation of the Republic had the confidence, intellect, and charisma to command armies that were willing to fight for them. Although the events surrounding the Gracchi brothers and Marius occurred a few years before Caesar was born, they set the stage for the grand entrance he would make.

Chapter 4

The Rome of Young Caesar

The years between the deaths of the Gracchi brothers, Marius's impact on the army, and Julius Caesar's birth in 100 B.C. foreshadowed the bloody struggle that would eventually define and occupy Caesar's entire life. Historians know his role in Roman history better than that of any other Roman figure. Caesar's character was born of the social struggle touched off by the Gracchi brothers, a generation before his birth. His political ambitions would eventually push that struggle to its ultimate height during the last years of his life.

Of the ambitious politicians of Caesar's era, only a few rose high enough to be remembered by history. Most floundered in the backwash of stronger men's ambitions. Weak politicians were swept along by the leadership and daring of the few great leaders, such as

Marius, Sulla, Pompey, Cicero, Marc Antony, and Octavian.

These Republican leaders all remain famous, yet the fame of Gaius Julius Caesar stands out above all the others. So great was the power and majesty of this one man that his name became associated with power and authority in several languages. So extraordinary was Caesar's impact on Roman politics that, two thousand years ago, he created a legacy that exists to this day in many Western civilizations.

Caesar's fame arose from his remarkable ability to do many things exceptionally well. Many of his contemporaries were one-dimensional men. Some were capable of leading soldiers into battle, or making crucial political decisions, or writing great works of literature. Caesar could do *all* of these things. He led soldiers in battle, delivered stirring speeches, made difficult decisions, wrote historical works documenting his wars, and had a keen understanding of human psychology. Caesar was a dominant leader for all time.

The Youth of Caesar

Caesar was born in Rome on either July 12 or 13, in the year 100 B.C., to his father, Gaius Julius Caesar, and his mother, Aurelia. Caesar's family was one of the relatively small number of old aristocratic families with a long history of involvement in Roman politics. Of the two political parties at this time, the Optimates and Populares, the family supported the political objectives of the Populares.

Julius Caesar grew up in Rome when it was still recovering from the bloody struggles caused by Marius and the Gracchi brothers.

From birth, there seems to have been a strong emotional attachment between Caesar and his mother. Caesar's father died in 85 B.C. when Caesar was only fifteen. He may not have been in Rome much during Caesar's youth.

Caesar was an only child who suffered from epileptic seizures. Later in his life, there were many difficult times either on the battlefield or while meeting with dignitaries in Rome when he suffered seizures that forced him to seek privacy. As for his appearance, the first-century Roman historian Suetonius related that

> Caesar is said to have been tall, fair, and well-built, with a rather broad face and keen, dark-brown eyes. . . . He was something of a dandy, always keeping his head carefully trimmed and shaved; and he has been accused of having certain other hairy parts of his body depilated with tweezers. His baldness was a disfigurement which his enemies harped upon . . . but he used to comb the thin strands of hair forward . . .[1]

Growing up in the cosmopolitan city of Rome taught Caesar a good deal about the different layers of Roman society. As a member of one of the old aristocratic families, his parents placed high expectations on him to excel in politics. However, his carousing in the streets also taught him that not all Roman youths lived privileged lives like his. His observations of people taught him how to move comfortably among all layers of society—a skill that would be invaluable in his later political career.

Like all boys born into one of the privileged families in Rome, Caesar grew up with a keen understanding of the struggles for power that went on in the city on an almost daily basis. With his exceptionally bright mind and quick wit, he observed other men's rise to power and carefully began to plan his own. For Caesar, both Marius and Sulla would prove to be role models for learning some of the ruthless tactics needed for success in Rome.

The Rise of Sulla

When King Jugurtha's army had surrendered after Marius's attack, Jugurtha himself arranged to surrender to Lucius Cornelius Sulla, who then handed him over to Marius. Unlike Marius, Sulla was an Optimate who seized on his minor success to take credit for the entire war. A cunning politician always hungry for advantage, Sulla used his moment of glory to turn against Marius. Claiming that he alone deserved credit for Jugurtha's defeat, Sulla exaggerated his own achievements while diminishing those of Marius.

A deadly rivalry flared between these two strong-willed leaders. Sulla felt that Marius had unfairly received all the credit for Jugurtha's defeat, when he himself had been involved in Jugurtha's surrender. Relations between the two leaders continued to worsen when the Optimates sought to give all the credit for defeating Jugurtha to Sulla.

When another war broke out in 88 B.C. against Mithradates VI, king of Pontus—an area in what is today northeastern Turkey—a dispute arose between Marius and Sulla over who should command the army needed to fight this war. Seeking to eliminate his hated rival, Sulla borrowed Marius's strategy. He raised his own army with the promise of rewards and then marched on Rome to destroy Marius. This was the first time a Roman general had entered the city to impose his own will on Rome. Marius, caught off guard by Sulla's bold advance, fled for Africa.

At this point, the old aristocratic families must have had some idea that the social climate in Rome was changing. First, the rebellions of the Gracchi brothers had taken place. Now, Roman armies—loyal to their leaders rather than to the Senate—were converging on the city. This must have been unsettling to the old aristocrats. Try as the Optimates might to maintain the control over Roman politics they had enjoyed for the previous four centuries, the last century of the Roman Republic would see the unraveling of their authority by the Populares.

The First Civil War

Now that both Marius and Sulla had their own private armies, head-to-head conflict was not far off. Shortly after Sulla's unprecedented show of force in Rome, he set out for Pontus to defeat Mithradates. In his absence, Marius returned from Africa. Joining forces with one of the consuls, Lucius Cornelius Cinna, Marius entered Rome unopposed by any of Sulla's supporters. Without much opposition from the Optimates, Marius and Cinna took charge of the city. They arranged to have themselves elected to the two consulships that year. Then, in the most vindictive show of violence since the murder of the Gracchi brothers and their followers, Marius ordered the murder of many of the Optimates in the city.

At this same time, Marius recognized that his teenage nephew, Julius Caesar, had the potential to become a leading political figure. Marius appointed Caesar to the office of *flamen dialis*, a member of the Roman priesthood. This appointment identified Caesar with his uncle's Populares politics.

Two years later, in 84 B.C., Caesar married Cinna's daughter, Cornelia, after he divorced his first wife. This politically motivated marriage, which resulted in the birth of a daughter named Julia, further confirmed Caesar's alliance with the Populares and thrust him deeper into the quicksand of Roman politics.

Following the elimination of many of Sulla's followers and the launching of Caesar's political career, Marius died of old age. Cinna was left in control of a city that had little to look forward to except Sulla's return after his victory over Mithradates. Cinna did not have long to wait.

In 83 B.C., Sulla returned to Rome at the head of his forty-thousand-man army. He was now completely unwilling to show any mercy toward his rivals. Cinna, barely able to muster any opposition to Sulla, was murdered by his own troops. Sulla now headed the only army in Rome. He could rule the city without opposition.

His first order of business was to take revenge on the Populares. The first-century historian Plutarch described Sulla's savage revenge:

> Sulla now devoted himself entirely to the work of butchery. The city was filled with murder and there was no counting the executions or setting a limit to them. Many people were killed because of purely personal ill feeling; they had no connexion with Sulla in any way, but Sulla, in order to gratify members of his own party, permitted them to be done away with. . . . Then immediately, and without consulting any magistrate, Sulla published a list of eighty men to be condemned. Public opinion was horrified, but, after a single day's interval, he published another list containing 220 more names, and next day a third list with the same number of names on it. And in a public speech . . . he said that he was publishing the names of all those whom he happened to remember: those who escaped his memory for the moment would have their names put up later. He also condemned anyone who sheltered or attempted to save a person whose name was on the lists. Death was the penalty for such acts of humanity, and there were no exceptions in the cases of brothers, sons, or parents.[2]

As a teenager, Caesar saw many of his family's friends killed by Sulla's henchmen and their property confiscated. Although Caesar himself was not targeted, Sulla ordered him to divorce his wife, Cornelia. Sulla hoped to break Caesar's connection with the Populares. Refusing the order to divorce, Caesar feared for his life. He decided to flee Rome until the political climate calmed down.

Sulla's Dictatorship

After murdering many of the leading Populares and declaring many more public enemies, Sulla proclaimed himself dictator of Rome. This position allowed him to rule without the checks and balances normally imposed by the Senate, consuls, and tribunes. As had been the case with Marius, Sulla now controlled his own army. No one dared to challenge his supreme position. As Professor Erich Gruen explained, the violence that preceded Sulla's dictatorship, involving Populares leaders such as the Gracchi brothers and Marius, "meant that the major decisions

The Roman Forum, where people met to engage in political debate.

were being made not in the forum [the place for public debate], the *curia* [the Senate House], or the *iudicia* [the courts], but on the battlefield. Sulla resolved to put an end to that cycle."[3]

According to Roman orator, statesman, and philosopher Cicero, the office of dictator was originally created as a way to cope with civil disturbances when the normal machinery of government worked too slowly. As such, the office was a legally constituted office that the Roman government had created for use in times of unusual crisis. The few dictators during the early years of the Republic usually held the office for just six months. Although Sulla was not the first man to use it, he set a dangerous example by maintaining his dictatorial powers until his retirement three years later in 79 B.C.

Sulla's intention in establishing the dictatorship was neither to muzzle the Senate nor to repress the bloody political rivalry among the aristocracy. Bare-knuckle politics had been a part of Republican strategy for hundreds of years. Rather, Sulla sought to end, once and for all, the bloody political fights that had produced alienated social reformers such as the Gracchi brothers and Marius, whose appeal to the general population threatened the tight grip the aristocratic families held on Rome.

If Roman politicians had learned anything about the basics of Roman politics from the violent behavior of Marius and Sulla, it was that the political stability of Rome lay not in the hands of the government but in the hands of the army. The Roman Senate, that old fortress for aristocratic families, had failed to support the basic needs of the poor soldiers. This failure provided an opportunity for clever leaders such as Marius and Sulla to manipulate the armies. Control of Rome was now available to whomever could promise land and money to the legions in exchange for their loyalty. Never before had Roman legions fought fellow Roman legions within the walls of the city. This dangerous situation would prevent the armies from ever again owing their allegiance to Rome.

The common people of Rome—the small farmers, the soldiers, and the urban poor—who lost their lives during this violent period did so to try and improve their quality of life. Their leaders, however, had other motives. Since all of them came from aristocratic families, they were more keenly focused on their individual success and the success of their political party—Populares or Optimates—than on the needs of the common people. Professor Erich Gruen made this observation of the times: "Struggles in the streets were basically extensions of struggles among Rome's prominent figures."[4]

Chapter 5

Caesar's Rise to Power

In 78 B.C., after Sulla's retirement, Julius Caesar felt it was safe to return to Rome. He entered the political arena and gained initial fame by successfully prosecuting two men who had been supporters of Sulla. Following these two legal victories, Caesar's reputation as an orator and politician was born. Wishing for even greater success as a prosecutor, Caesar traveled to the island of Rhodes in the eastern Aegean Sea in 75 B.C., when he was twenty-five years old, to hone his rhetorical skills under the famous orator Apollonius Molon.

While sailing to Rhodes, pirates captured Caesar's ship and held him for ransom for almost forty days. Upon hearing that his ransom would be twenty talents, a fairly large sum, Caesar laughed derisively at the amount. He demanded that it be raised to fifty talents because of his importance. Contemptuous of the pirates, he threatened to crucify them as soon as they released him. True to his word, following his release after the ransom had been paid, he immediately raised a fleet of ships, pursued the pirates, and crucified them all.

Arrogance such as this was a hallmark of Caesar's character. Throughout his career as a general and

Source Document

When these men first demanded of him twenty talents for his ransom, he laughed at them for not understanding the value of their prisoner, and voluntarily engaged to give them fifty. He presently despatched those about him to several places to raise the money, till at last he was left among a set of the most bloodthirsty people in the world. . . . Yet he made so little of them, that when he had a mind to sleep, he would send to them, and order them to make no noise. For thirty-eight days, with all the freedom in the world, he amused himself with joining in their exercises and games, as if they had not been his keepers, but his guards. He wrote verses and speeches, and made them his auditors, and those who did not admire them, he called to their faces illiterate and barbarous. . . .[1]

Historian Plutarch described young Caesar's reckless treatment of his kidnappers.

politician, he often mocked his rivals with insulting comments about their character and capabilities. In so doing, he made his supporters see him as an extraordinarily confident and fearless leader. Through his entire life, Caesar never seemed to waver in his ambition and belief that destiny had great accomplishments in store for him. While serving in Spain at one point in his early career, Caesar came across a statue of Macedonian leader Alexander the Great and was overheard expressing his sorrow that, "at my age Alexander was already king over so many peoples, while I have never yet achieved anything really remarkable. . . ."[2]

Caesar, Crassus, and Pompey—An Alliance of Enemies

The three years of Sulla's dictatorship had given the citizens of Rome a much-needed rest from the vicious politics of the Optimates and Populares. They did not know, however, that this respite would be all too brief. The dark side of fate was not yet ready to release Rome from further turmoil. The few years after Sulla's retirement witnessed the rise of three men eager to fill the vacuum he had left. These three men—Gnaeus Pompey, Marcus Licinius Crassus, and Julius Caesar—would now dominate Roman politics.

Pompey was the most powerful and popular of the three leaders in Rome at the end of Sulla's dictatorship. Six years older than Caesar, Pompey was born to an aristocratic family. Growing up with the expectation that he would follow in his father's footsteps to the consulship, by the age of twenty-three, Pompey had fought on Sulla's side against the Populares faction led by Marius. In 84 B.C., he raised three legions and set out to destroy the remnants of Marius's army in Africa and Sicily. With Sulla in power after the civil war, Pompey's return to Rome was celebrated by a triumphal parade. He was honored with the title Pompey *Magnus*, meaning in Latin "Pompey the Great."

Between 76 and 71 B.C., Pompey gained greater military experience and fame by defeating scattered supporters of Marius in Spain. Many in Rome idolized Pompey, now thirty-five, as he took aim at higher political office. With his connection to Sulla and his military experience, Pompey was the best-positioned man to dominate Roman politics.

Crassus was born in 115 B.C. Like Pompey, he began his rise to power on the battlefield, fighting with Sulla against Marius. After the civil war, however, Crassus gained fame not in warfare but in finance. Following the defeat of Marius, many of his supporters lost their lives and property. Crassus made a fortune by scooping up much of this property. He continued to increase his fortune by loaning money at high interest rates until he had earned a reputation as the wealthiest man in Rome. Eager to show off his wealth, Crassus paid for lavish public dinner parties as well as a regular series of gladiator fights. In these contests, men fought to the death. Crassus also put on wild animal hunts to entertain the public. Stories about his wasteful habit of spending seemingly endless amounts of money were so common that his name became associated with vulgar and wasteful public displays of money.

At this time in Rome, no man could hope for a successful career in politics without an accomplished career in the military. In need of a military campaign to bolster his political ambitions and to improve his sleazy public image, Crassus seized on an opportunity to suppress a slave revolt in 73 B.C. Near the town of Capua, about one hundred miles south of Rome, several hundred slaves who were training to be gladiators escaped and fled throughout the neighboring regions. Led by a slave named Spartacus, their numbers

Influential Romans like Crassus showed off their wealth by holding popular events, such as gladiator fights.

swelled as more and more slaves joined the revolt. Within less than a year, the ranks of the slave rebellion had ballooned to ninety thousand and attempts to defeat them had failed. Crassus finally caught up with Spartacus in 71 B.C. and forced a pitched battle that finally defeated the slaves. Those not killed in battle were crucified at the sides of the road. Unfortunately for Crassus, many of Spartacus's supporters fled north, right into the hands of Pompey's army, which was returning from Spain. The rebels were killed. Pompey, ever the opportunist, seized on this bit of good fortune to claim the victory for himself. Historian Plutarch told Crassus's sad story:

> Crassus had had good fortune, had shown excellent generalship, and had risked his own life in the fighting; nevertheless the success of Crassus served to increase the fame of Pompey. The fugitives from the battle fell in with Pompey's troops and were destroyed, so that Pompey, in his dispatch to the senate, was able to say that, while Crassus certainly had conquered the slaves in open battle, he himself had dug the war up by the roots.[3]

Both Crassus and Pompey elevated their political status in Rome by successfully running for the two consulships in 70 B.C. Although these two men had many things in common, friendship for each other was not one of them. Their decision to run for election to the consulships and to support each other was motivated by nothing other than selfish ambition.

Of the three central political figures in Rome at this time, Caesar was the least qualified, the least known, and the most in need of support. Ironically, Caesar, whose support of the Populares party placed him in staunch opposition to these two Optimates leaders, busied himself supporting the election of Pompey and establishing a friendship with Crassus. In this regard, Caesar had at least one thing in common with Pompey and Crassus: He, too, was motivated by selfishness. He would do whatever was necessary to further his own political ambitions, even create alliances with bitter enemies if it would help. And indeed it did. The following year, in 69 B.C., Caesar was elected to the office of quaestor, one of the officers in charge of the treasury. In 62 B.C., he was elected a praetor, a high-ranking judge.

To win the needed votes, Caesar borrowed huge sums of money, promoting gladiatorial games as a way of advertising his candidacy. Unconcerned with repayment of his massive debt, Caesar finished his office as praetor in 61 B.C. and departed for the province of Spain, of which the Senate had made him governor. When Caesar's creditors saw him ready to leave, they descended on him, thinking they might never see him again. They demanded their money and prevented him from leaving. Since Caesar did not have the money to pay his debts, he borrowed money from his new friend Crassus.

All three of the men in this unlikely alliance believed that the Senate owed them special favors for the wars they had won. However, when Pompey returned to Rome in 61 B.C., after his many successes, the Senate refused his requests to recognize his victories publicly or to give land to his veterans as a reward for their battles. Pompey was furious. The Senate had also rebuffed Crassus when he requested that it remove a bad debt incurred by several of his friends. Added to this list of angry men was Caesar. On returning from his year as governor of Spain, he requested a triumphal parade through Rome and an opportunity to run for the consulship. The Senate rejected these requests, just as they had the requests of Pompey and

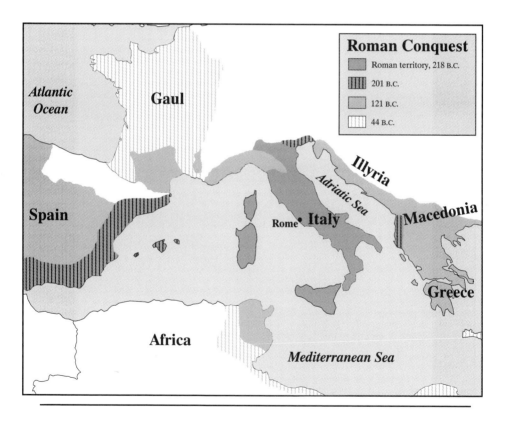

Rome continued to expand its power despite the struggles among its political leaders. This map shows Roman conquests to 44 B.C.

Crassus. The Senate had driven the three men into each other's arms.

The First Triumvirate—Power Brokers

The jockeying for political dominance among these three men became obvious to all of Rome, and it sent tremors through the city. Most Romans remembered the terrible bloodletting between Marius and Sulla twenty years earlier. Everyone could see that, once again, the political cauldron was beginning to boil over. Not only were there clear tensions between the political aspirations of Caesar, Pompey, and Crassus, but there was also a host of lesser men now coming forward like scavengers, ready and eager to gnaw on the carrion left behind by these three. Professor H. H. Scullard saw the period this way:

> . . . few [of the Optimates and Populares] were striving for anything other than personal power: mostly they were devoid of higher motives, and if on occasion they appealed to certain aspects of [freedom] . . . it was for their personal ends rather than for the . . . commonwealth.[4]

Stinging from the Senate's refusal to grant their requests, Caesar, Pompey, and Crassus realized that, individually, none of them could force the hand of the Senate. As a group, however, each might be able to get what he wanted.

In 60 B.C., after returning from his term as governor of Spain, Caesar met with Pompey and Crassus to strike an informal agreement. This agreement, called the First Triumvirate, had no legal foundation, yet the three men, who collectively held more power than their opponents, used it to thumb their noses at the Senate and to carve up the Roman provinces among themselves. With this private agreement, each man supported the needs of the others in order to get what he wanted himself. Without any high-minded principles, each member of the triumvirate strove to win personal power and status.

Pompey got the settlement he had negotiated after his victories in the eastern Mediterranean, a triumphal parade through Rome to celebrate his military victory, and land for his veterans. Crassus received the debt cancellation he had sought for several of his friends. Caesar's reward was the consulship in 59 B.C., despite Optimates hostility. In 58 B.C., he was appointed governor of Gaul, part of modern-day France.

To cement their relationship further, Caesar gave his daughter Julia to Pompey in marriage. With the support of Pompey and Crassus, Caesar headed for Gaul after his one-year term as consul.

By this time, the public saw what the triumvirs had in mind. People began to call them the Three-Headed Monster. Politics in Rome became increasingly sinister. Each of the triumvirs watched the moves of the other two, not trusting anyone. Bands of political thugs ran through the streets of Rome, roughing up political opponents and threatening to harm senators if they did not cast their votes as they were told. As disreputable as politics had been in the past, the climate was getting worse.

Caesar and the Gaulic Wars

In 58 B.C., Caesar left Rome and proceeded north to Gaul to become its governor. At that time, a tribe called the Helvetii had crossed into the Roman province without the permission of the Roman Senate, and a German tribe called the Aedui had invaded Gaulic territory. Apparently, Caesar's goal was to expel these two tribes and to calm the province. Caesar, however, knowing that Pompey and Crassus were not to be trusted regardless of their triumvirate agreement, also needed to build up an army and enough political prestige so that he could secure re-election as consul on his return to Rome.

Caesar marched into Gaul with six legions, defeated the Helvetii, and forced them to return to their home area one hundred miles away. Next, he crushed the Aedui forces. By 57 B.C., Caesar had recaptured all of northern Gaul and had crushed one last revolt of the Gauls, led by Vercingetorix, in 52 B.C.

Gaul was Caesar's proving ground as an extremely talented general, far superior to either Pompey or Crassus. He understood strategy and tactics, and he could command the respect of his gritty foot soldiers. He was always aware of the movements of his enemies. With his great skill and daring, Caesar consistently outmaneuvered and defeated them.

While fighting in Gaul, Caesar dictated a history of the wars called *De Bello Gallico*, meaning "About the Gaulic War." Of all the military leaders of this period, only Caesar was an author. In this history of his fighting in Gaul, Caesar described the land and the different tribes and their cultures. He also provided a detailed narrative of his army's activities and his own military strategies.

It was while Caesar was in Gaul that he acquired his reputation as a superior strategist and soldier who often risked his own life in hand-to-hand combat at the head of his attacking soldiers. The Roman historian Suetonius explained: "Caesar was a most skilful swordsman and horseman. . . . He always led his army, more often on foot than in the saddle . . . and could travel for long distances at incredible speed. . . ."[5]

While he was in Gaul, Caesar's personal friends continued to dominate politics in Rome. This, however, threatened Pompey's position. It became necessary for the triumvirs to arrange a meeting at Luca in 56 B.C., which brought about a temporary reconciliation. It was decided that Caesar would continue as governor in Gaul for another five years, while Pompey and Crassus would both be consuls for 55 B.C. Caesar then went off to raid Britain and returned to Gaul to suppress yet another tribal revolt. Crassus, ever eager for military glory, went to his post in Syria in northern Africa.

A Crumbling Triumvirate

It was clear by now that Crassus was the weak link of the triumvirate. He had failed to gain the military and political power base that Pompey and Caesar now held. As events unfolded, it was becoming clear that the renewal of the Optimates-Populares struggle

Source Document

. . . There is a river [called] the Saone, which flows through the territories of the Aedui and Sequani into the Rhone with such incredible slowness, that it can not be determined by the eye in which direction it flows. This the Helvetii were crossing by rafts and boats joined together. When Caesar was informed by spies that the Helvetii had already conveyed three parts of their forces across that river, but that the fourth part was left behind on this side of the Saone, he set out from camp with three legions during the third watch, and came up with that division which had not yet crossed the river. Attacking them encumbered with baggage, and not expecting him, he cut to pieces a great part of them; the rest betook themselves to flight. . . .[6]

Caesar was not only a great general, but also a good writer, who wrote his own accounts of the wars he fought.

would most likely be played out between Pompey and Caesar. Never as aggressive or dominant as Caesar or Pompey, Crassus did serve to hold the triumvirate together and helped keep the peace between Pompey and Caesar. Caesar's daughter Julia, who was still married to Pompey, had a similar effect. The two of them acted as buffers, keeping Caesar and Pompey from renewing the civil war fought thirty years earlier between Marius and Sulla.

As fate would have it, two years after the renewal of the triumvirate at Luca, Julia died. One year later, Crassus was defeated and killed in battle against the Parthians, who lived in the present-day country of Iran. These two events removed the last two buffers keeping Caesar and Pompey from destroying each other.

With Crassus out of the way and the bond of marriage removed, Caesar continued to subdue more territory in Gaul and Britain, while Pompey had Rome to himself. Although this fact gave him a distinct advantage over Caesar, he failed to control the rowdy mobs of Caesar's supporters that ran through the city. Pompey came under the influence of the old Optimates families that wanted to put an end to Caesar and the entire Populares movement. As tensions mounted in Rome, many desperately sought a compromise that would avoid another civil war. No such luck was to be found.

Caesar was ordered by a vote of the Senate to disband his army, which was spending the winter at a small town near the Rubicon River, the boundary separating the province of Gaul from central Italy, and return to Rome. On January 7, 49 B.C., the Senate, acting to support Pompey, declared Caesar a public enemy. All activity in Rome froze in time as everyone waited to see whether Caesar would disband his army and return to Rome alone or whether, in defiance of the Senate, he would return with his army intent on war. Caesar made them wait only one week.

A Clash of Titans—Caesar Versus Pompey

Crossing the Rubicon on January 14, Caesar and his legions swept south toward Rome. Caesar crossed the river in defiance of the Senate with the single-minded purpose of smashing Pompey and his Optimates allies.

As had been the case for many generations, Caesar, like Pompey, was largely motivated by considerations of personal power and prestige. Caesar openly declared on many occasions that his personal dignity was more important to him than life itself. It would, however, be unfair to assume that Caesar's troops had the same motive. The common soldiers knew nothing about personal power and prestige, but they did know a great deal about poverty and political oppression. From their standpoint, Caesar would reward them with money and land for crossing the Rubicon and crushing Pompey.

Some modern historians have argued that Caesar and his legions intended to destroy the Republic once and for all. Professor Erich Gruen, however, observed: "The Roman army consisted of individuals interested in profit and social betterment; it was not a source of revolutionary sentiment. Not even the soldiers of Julius Caesar marched into Italy with the intent or the desire to bring down the Roman Republic."[1]

Caesar Approaches Rome

When news of Caesar's approach reached Rome, the population panicked at the thought of Caesar's and Pompey's armies clashing in the city's streets. Many remembered the terror and bloodshed at the hands of the armies of Marius and Sulla a generation earlier. As the panic spread, Pompey decided to abandon Rome, to the dismay of his allies. He believed that, in so doing, he could cut off Caesar from his supplies and remaining troops and starve them into submission.

As Caesar marched toward Rome, Pompey gave the order to abandon the city to go to the seaport of Brindisi, 325 miles southeast of Rome. He hoped the new location would give him an advantage in case he needed to flee to the safety of Greece. This further irritated his supporters, since only a few months earlier, Pompey had bragged, "I have only to stamp on the soil of Italy for cavalry and infantry to rise from the ground."[2] Now Caesar was doing the stamping.

Always the more ingenious of the two men, Caesar was busily capturing Pompey's soldiers and adding them to his own army as he approached Rome. His clever tactic was to offer them forgiveness for fighting against him if they would join him. Never before had Roman soldiers had their lives spared in this way. Caesar used these opportunities to advertise that he was a fair and reasonable leader who sought a peaceful resolution to this crisis.

Cicero, the great Roman statesman and orator, sided with Pompey. Still, he tried hard to negotiate a settlement between the two leaders. He genuinely believed that the Republic needed to be preserved at all costs. Negotiations failed, however, when Pompey and his supporters fled Brindisi for Greece on March 17.

As the opposition melted away, Caesar entered Rome and began to consolidate his authority. To win over citizens, Caesar offered free grain and money to all Romans and continued to seek a peaceful resolution through negotiations with Pompey.

Not all his actions, however, showed kindness. In need of money, Caesar learned that when Pompey had fled Rome, he had neglected to take the national treasury with him. Caesar headed straight for the temple of Saturn in the Roman Forum, where the money was kept, and demanded all of it. The tribune Lucius Metellus blocked Caesar's entry to the temple and refused to hand over the treasure. This defiance, which was perfectly legal on Metellus's part, placed Caesar in the unpopular position of threatening the tribune's life. As the two men stood face-to-face at the doors of the temple, Caesar told Metellus that it would he far easier to run a sword through him than to stand there arguing with him. At this threat of violence, Metellus stepped aside. Caesar's troops plundered the entire national treasure—fifteen thousand bars of gold, thirty thousand bars of silver, and 30 million coins.[3] This act soured the followers of the Populares, who had thought that Caesar's ethics placed him above such illegal behavior. Now, fully in control of Rome but having failed to make peace with Pompey, Caesar turned his attention to the coming civil war.

Pharsalus—The Final Clash

Before Caesar could pursue Pompey in Greece, he first needed to defeat Pompey's army in Spain to prevent it from invading Rome in his absence. Although Pompey was not with his troops in Spain, they were still a threat to Caesar. Disdainful of Pompey's military abilities, the Roman historian Suetonius wrote that, before Caesar departed for Spain, he arrogantly told his staff, "I am off to meet an army without a leader; when I return I shall meet a leader without an army."[4] After defeating Pompey's troops in Spain, Caesar cast his gaze toward Pompey and his supporters in Greece.

Across the Adriatic Sea in Greece, Pompey—along with two hundred senators who were loyal Optimates followers—was busy assembling an army of forty thousand soldiers, nine thousand cavalry, and a navy

When Rome invaded Greece during its expansion, the Romans took care not to destroy the great architecture, showing their sincere respect for Greek culture and accomplishments. Now Pompey fled to Greece for safety.

of three hundred warships. To stop Pompey's military buildup, Caesar hurried to Greece with seven legions during the winter of 48 B.C. The next spring, Marc Antony—a significant ally who had been one of Caesar's trusted lieutenants during the Gaulic wars— joined Caesar with four more legions, bringing Caesar's total strength to about twenty-five thousand infantry and fourteen hundred cavalry.

After a few weeks of skirmishing and maneuvering, the two large armies met on the plains of Pharsalus, located in central Greece, for the final clash. Although

Pompey had a significant numerical advantage and had chosen the battlefield, Caesar had the advantage of years of experience fighting in Gaul and Spain. He also had a confident personality and was willing to gamble. He was a great believer in luck. He once said, "Luck is the greatest power in all things and especially in war."[5]

As soon as the two armies collided, it was evident to everyone that Caesar had outmaneuvered his rival. Before the day ended, Pompey saw the slaughter of six thousand of his troops and many of the senators who had thrown their support to his cause. As he fled from the field of battle, he saw another twenty-four thousand of his troops surrounded and captured by Caesar's men.

Not bothering to regroup, Pompey fled to Egypt, where he believed he would be safe. In this regard, he found no more success than he had at Pharsalus. In fact, he found less. As soon as Pompey waded ashore from his boat, he was murdered by Egyptians under the orders of King Ptolemy, who hoped to demonstrate allegiance to Caesar. When Caesar reached Egypt two months later, these same Egyptians handed him a cloth sack as soon as his ship landed. Opening the sack, Caesar recoiled in horror. The sack held the head of Pompey. Stunned, Caesar went off by himself to grieve Pompey's death, a man who had been a mortal enemy as well as a lifelong acquaintance.

In keeping with his policy of forgiveness, Caesar agreed to forgive all those who had fought against him if they would surrender their weapons and return to Italy. Despite this generous offer, many troops remained loyal to Pompey's cause and scattered throughout the Mediterranean. Instead of hurrying back to Rome to take command of the city, Caesar spent the next six months in Egypt, firming up his grip on this important country and the surrounding area. Egypt was a key territory. It provided most of the grain needed to feed the population of Rome. Civil unrest between Ptolemy and his sister Cleopatra, however, threatened the peace in Egypt. Caesar knew that, if he did not take the time to settle the strife in this area, war would break out again as soon as he left for Rome.

Caesar was forced to choose sides in Egypt's problems. He decided to support Cleopatra against her brother because she had the stronger political position. Following a brief civil war, the combined forces of Caesar and Cleopatra defeated Ptolemy, whose body was dumped into the Nile River.

For the next two months, much to the displeasure of many of his supporters, Caesar and Cleopatra leisurely sailed the Nile River. The result of this liaison was a son named Caesarion born to Cleopatra after Caesar had returned to Rome. (Caesar's wife, Cornelia, had died around 68 B.C.) This union was the first, but certainly not the last, that Cleopatra would have with Roman leaders.

Although Caesar had been away from Rome for nearly a year, he had placed his trusted friend Marc Antony in charge of the city in his absence. While

Caesar remained in Egypt, he was nominated for dictator in Rome for a one-year term. During this year, Caesar was free to pass whatever laws he wished without interference from the Senate, consuls, or tribunes.

Caesar's Dictatorship

Caesar finally returned during the summer of 47 B.C. After making peace with Cicero, he headed to Rome to cement his authority before departing for the North African coast, where survivors of Pompey's forces were gathering. Politicians who had supported Caesar's cause against Pompey were rewarded with Senate offices and other positions. His loyal soldiers received rewards of money and land, and were then released from service. The poor in Rome were given free rents for one year and interest on loans was reduced.

Once again firmly in control and still popular with most Romans, Caesar set sail for North Africa to destroy what was left of Pompey's forces during the winter of 47 B.C. At the Battle of Thapsus, Caesar once again showed his military genius by defeating forces loyal to Pompey's son, Sextus, and one of Pompey's closest friends, Cato.

At the Battle of Thapsus, a coastal town, one of Caesar's most remarkable flashes of genius occurred. While nearing the coast by ship, Caesar was sensitive to the fact that Roman soldiers hated traveling by boat. They preferred the safety of land. In fact, Roman generals would often march their men great distances rather than risk even a short boat ride.

As Caesar's fleet approached shallow water, the order was given to prepare to jump over the side of the ships. Caesar sensed that all eyes were glued on him as he stood on the prow of his ship, ready to be the first to hit the beach. When he jumped to the sand, he stumbled and fell face down in the shallows. Horrified at seeing their leader falter, none of the superstitious soldiers obeyed the order to vault over the sides of their ships into the surf. Caesar, aware of the soldiers' refusal to follow their stumbling leader, quickly spun around to face his fleet. As he stood up, he grabbed two hands full of sand and raised them above his head for all to see. He yelled to his soldiers, "Africa, I hold you in my hands."[6] With that stroke of genius, the soldiers thought that Caesar had intentionally fallen on the sand to make a dramatic gesture of conquest. They leaped over the sides of their ships and stormed the beach.

Having finally crushed all remnants of Pompey's African support, Caesar returned to Rome. He was greeted by renewed fanfare from his loyal followers. Senators friendly to Caesar appointed him dictator again—this time for ten years, rather than the usual one year. Flushed with victory and a sense of invincibility, Caesar gave cash gifts to his veterans and smaller amounts to all Roman citizens. In keeping with his reputation for granting forgiveness, Caesar pardoned dozens of his former enemies. Around

February 44 B.C., he was honored with the title *dictator perpetuus,* or dictator for life. Caesar now set to the task of passing a series of reforms aimed at improving the administration of Rome.

Caesar the Reformer

After four years of stubborn conflict ranging the length and breadth of the Mediterranean, Caesar had finally defeated Pompey's supporters. During this civil war, the citizens of Rome saw very little of Caesar. At the age of fifty-five and true to his Populares leanings, he now turned his attention to the reforms he had promised his followers. As was the case with everything else he undertook, he approached his reforms with an energy and creativity that assured success.

Immediately following the ruinous civil war, many of Caesar's legions were threatening to mutiny if they were not properly rewarded for their loyal participation. To exert his authority over them and to scale back their demands, Caesar shamed them by addressing them as citizens rather than as soldiers. As soon as they heard this, they ceased their complaints and obeyed him. As a reward for their loyalty, Caesar paid each man a sum of money and established twenty new colonies in Greece, North Africa, Gaul, and Northern Italy as farms for them. Caesar chose these colonies because the land was cheap and because it was an effective way of controlling distant areas by spreading Roman culture. In addition to his veterans, eighty thousand families accepted Caesar's offer to colonize.

Caesar also addressed the problem of high public debt by lowering interest rates and by canceling one fourth of all public debt.

Caesar also understood the importance of creating a lasting peace in Gaul, Spain, and North Africa. Wars in these areas had been costly to Rome. Caesar demonstrated his creative genius by making them provinces and extending Roman citizenship to many of the leading families. By this gesture of friendship, these people looked on Rome with kinder feelings than in the past. They grew to appreciate the benefits of citizenship. To provide a fertile foundation on which Roman culture would mature, Caesar drew up municipal laws to govern the new towns and to provide security for their people. These laws become the cornerstone for municipal and provincial administration, which lasted until the fall of the Roman Empire, five hundred years later.

Within Rome, Caesar saw that there was much work to be done. Caesar spent lavish amounts of money on building programs. Among his projects was the construction of a new forum named after Caesar himself, the Forum Julius. He also built libraries and temples, established major road repair programs, and created a new harbor at the port city of Ostia.

Caesar also recognized that Rome, as the major Mediterranean power, needed more senators to assist with new laws. He enlarged Senate membership from six hundred to nine hundred, including many new citizens from the Roman provinces. Since many of these men were his friends and allies, he strengthened his own control over this governing body.

As the undisputed master of Rome, Caesar received many honors. The seventh month of the year, Quinctilis, was renamed Julius (July). Statues of Caesar were erected by the hundreds. Coins were struck bearing his likeness. Holidays were dedicated in his honor, and triumphal parades were held throughout Rome to honor his military victories.

Whether Caesar took all this adulation seriously is a matter of some dispute. In mid-February 44 B.C., when he officially acquired the title of dictator for life, he needed no other power or other titles. He could now control the tribunes, dominate the Senate, and behave as he wished before the common people. Many enemies spread rumors that he was behaving more like a king than a Roman leader. Upon his return from a festival, he is said to have remarked, "I am not king, but Caesar—*non sum rex sed Caesar.*"[7]

Caesar had, in effect, achieved precisely what the Roman people had hated for most of their long history, the dictatorial behavior of the ancient kings. Some historians, however, do not see Caesar's dictatorship for life as an attempt to act as an unreasonable king. Rather, they see his dictatorship as a temporary necessity to restore order to the war-torn Republic before returning authority back to the consuls, Senate, and the people. He certainly had not crossed the Rubicon in 49 B.C. to fight a four-year civil war to allow the Republic to fall back into the chaos of war.

The Roman people showed their support for Caesar with triumphal parades such as this one.

Source Document

Oh, what a formidable guest to have had! . . . the whole establishment was so crowded with soldiers that even the room where Caesar himself was to dine could hardly be kept clear from them; it is a fact that there were two thousand men! . . . And certainly everything was very good, and well served; nay more, I may say that

> "Though the cook was good,
> 'Twas Attic salt that flavoured best the food."

There were three dining-rooms besides, where there was a very hospitable reception for the gentlemen of his suite; while the inferior class of freedmen and slaves had abundance at any rate; for as to the better class, they had a more refined table. In short, I think I acquitted myself like a man. The guest however was not the sort of person to whom you would say "I shall be most delighted if you will come here again on your way back"; once is enough.[8]

Cicero, who opposed Caesar's dictatorship, gave this account of a dinner Caesar attended.

Whatever Caesar might have had in mind for the future of the Roman Republic will forever be a matter of debate. Despite all his loyal followers, some of the old Optimates families were convinced that Caesar would never give up his dictatorship. Viewing Caesar as a tyrant who would never restore the authority of the Senate and the aristocratic families, several of the Optimates families who had been loyal to Pompey began to form a plot.

The Ides of March

Unknown to Caesar, leaders of a conspiracy to assassinate him chose March 15, the Ides of March on the Roman calendar, to take action. Led by Gaius Cassius and Marcus Brutus, two men Caesar knew well, the sixty conspirators decided to slay him during a session of the Senate. The plan was for each of the sixty men involved in the plot to bring a dagger to the Senate that day. At a signal, they would surround Caesar and kill him.

The men's reasons for joining the conspiracy were varied. Some feared that Caesar would never relinquish his power back to the Republican form of government. Some remained loyal to Pompey's memory and wanted Caesar dead. Others had personal quarrels with Caesar.

On the morning of the Ides of March, Caesar's third wife, Calpurnia, was unusually concerned for her husband's well-being. (Caesar had married her in 59 B.C. with the hope of having a male child to whom he could pass on his political position. Calpurnia, however, bore him no children in the years they were married.) Fearing for his life as a result of a dream she had had the night before, she begged him to send someone else to the Senate in his place or at least to take his bodyguards with him. Dreams played an important role in the lives of many Romans. Following unusual dreams, Romans often called upon interpreters of dreams who would explain their meaning. Many Romans made important decisions based on dream interpretations.

Close advisors to Caesar were concerned that there might be an attempt on his life. They, too, urged him to take bodyguards. Caesar, however, dismissed their concerns as he had done before, saying, "There is nothing more unfortunate than a permanent guard, which is a sign of ever present fear. It is better to die once than to be always expecting death."[9] Unaware of the plot, Caesar entered Pompey's theater, where the Senate was scheduled to meet that day, and took a seat while the senators assembled.

At an agreed-upon signal, the conspirators quietly surrounded Caesar without his noticing that anything unusual was happening. These were, after all, men with whom Caesar had associated for many years. He counted many of them as his friends. After a moment of hesitation that froze the conspirators in time, Caesar suddenly sensed that something was terribly wrong. As Caesar rose from his chair as if to make ready for whatever fate was about to deal him, Caesar saw the conspirators close in. The Roman historian Suetonius told the infamous story:

> Tillius Cimber . . . came up close, pretending to ask a question. Caesar made a gesture of postponement, but Cimber caught hold of his shoulders. "This is violence!" Caesar cried, and at that moment, one of the Casca brothers . . . stabbed him just below the throat. Caesar grasped Casca's arm and ran it through with his stylus [a pointed stick]; he was leaping away when another dagger caught him in the breast. Confronted by a ring of drawn daggers, he drew the top of his gown over his face. . . . Twenty-three dagger thrusts went home as he stood there . . . some say that when he saw Marcus Brutus about to deliver the second blow, he reproached him in Greek with: "You, too, my son?"[10]

As Caesar lay bleeding to death on the floor, the assassins ran through the streets of Rome, proclaiming the liberation of the city. At this point, Cicero, who had opposed Caesar yet had refused to take part in the assassination, joined their ranks.

The assassins believed that, by murdering Caesar, they would be hailed as heroes for reinstating the former glory of the Republic. They could not have been more wrong. They failed to understand that the majority of the common people would not enthusiastically receive a return to the Republic of the Optimates.

When Caesar's funeral arrangements had been announced, tens of thousands of people flocked to the Roman Forum to hear the eulogy delivered by Marc Antony from the *Rostrum* (a large platform similar to a stage from which orators and politicians delivered

Powerful and well-loved leaders like Julius Caesar were honored after death with a public cremation.

speeches to the public). They also hoped to catch a glimpse of the great man before his cremation. First-century historian Plutarch described Antony's eulogy:

> It so happened that when Caesar's body was carried out for burial, Antony delivered the customary eulogy over it in the Forum. When he saw that his oratory had cast a spell over the people and that they were deeply stirred by his words, he began to introduce into his praises a note of pity and of indignation at Caesar's fate. Finally, at the close of his speech, he snatched up the dead man's robe and brandished it aloft, all bloodstained as it was and stabbed through in many places, and called those who had done the deed murderers and villains.[11]

So stirred were the listeners that, as Caesar's body slowly moved through the crowd, the sight of the stilled body of the almost mythical leader began to generate a dramatic effect on the people. In a matter of minutes, the orderly throng began to surge closer in order to touch their dead leader. In a flash, voices shouted for twigs and pieces of wood to start a funeral pyre. Before order could be restored, the unruly crowd had spontaneously dragged the body of Caesar from the bearers and threw it on the burning pyre, cremating him on the spot.

Chapter 7

The Final Agony— Octavian Versus Antony

Had one lived at this time in Roman history, having endured the vicious struggle between the Optimates and Populares, followed by the ruinous civil war between Caesar and Pompey, and finally the bloody assassination of Caesar, one might have thought that a repeat of these events would be very unlikely. However, Rome's struggles were not over. As Roman historian H. H. Scullard observed, "Caesar himself is said to have remarked [that] his removal would merely involve the Republic in further troubles and civil wars."[1]

The fact that the civil war had ended and that both Pompey and Caesar were dead did not mean that the reasons for the war had gone away. All along the corridors of power in the Roman Forum, the old guard

Optimates, led by Cicero, spoke of the restoration of the Republic. At the same time, the Populares, led by Marc Antony, jockeyed to position themselves to fill Caesar's shoes. Despite the differences between these two political camps, one fact had not changed: All contenders for power continued to be driven selfishly by their quest for power and prestige.

Caesar's death created a power vacuum that begged to be filled, either by those loyal to him or by those who had murdered him. Both sides eagerly stepped forward.

Caesar's Successors

Supporters of Caesar included his old friends Marc Antony, who had fought with him in Gaul and against Pompey, and Marcus Lepidus, governor of part of Gaul and Spain. Of the two men, Antony was the one more likely to assume Caesar's mantle of greatness. Although Antony was a man of flawed character known for extravagant living as a youth, he had spent much of his time with Caesar during the civil war. The assassins had considered killing Antony along with Caesar but decided that it would not be necessary—an oversight they later regretted. Lepidus, although not as close with Caesar as Antony had been, had his army ready should fighting break out in Rome.

To these two supporters of Caesar, fate would soon add a third. Following Caesar's death, the reading of his will revealed his request for the distribution of various sums of money to individuals, soldiers, and to the citizens of Rome. This much had been anticipated. What came as a shock to everyone, however, was Caesar's deathbed adoption of his great-nephew, Octavian, as his son and the heir to his position. No one who knew Caesar could have forecasted such a move, but Caesar must have seen some quality in the young man that moved him to adopt Octavian. Caesar also left Octavian three quarters of his personal fortune. This twist of fate devastated Antony more than anyone else. He had hoped to take over Caesar's undisputed position as leader of the Populares.

The Boy

Just nineteen years old, Octavian had been training in the military when the news of Caesar's death reached him. As soon as he learned that he had been adopted, he changed his name to Gaius Julius Caesar to advertise his connection with Caesar. Then he struck out for Rome.

Arriving in April, about one month after the assassination, Octavian received a warm welcome from Caesar's legions and from many of Caesar's old friends. Since Antony was the most respected of Caesar's loyal friends, it was not surprising that Octavian turned to him for guidance. It did not take long, however, for Octavian to realize that Antony was irritated at his arrival in Rome and was taking a position against him.

Older in experience than his youthful face suggested, Octavian, dubbed "the boy" by many senators, quickly showed his political savvy by appealing to Caesar's veteran troops for support against his rivals. If Octavian had thought that his opposition would come from Pompey's supporters who had assassinated Caesar, he quickly learned that his true enemy, Antony, was close to him. By virtue of his name, which connected him to Caesar, Octavian had a magical charm that no rival could claim. Several of Antony's legions immediately declared their allegiance to him.

Seeing a possible ally in the youthful Octavian, Cicero and many of Pompey's followers approached him and proposed an alliance against Antony. Cicero considered the boy a valuable weapon against Antony who could later be disposed of easily. This attitude was decidedly shortsighted. Although Octavian willingly turned against Antony, the notion of being aligned with the party of Cassius and Brutus, the two men who were most identified with the death of Caesar, was unacceptable.

The leading politicians of Rome, whether they were Optimates or Populares, could not have foreseen the extraordinary strength of character within this teenager. Standing in Rome with eight of Caesar's legions, Octavian, following in the footsteps of Sulla and Caesar, demanded and received the office of consul for the year 43 B.C. Now there were three men of extraordinary power in Rome: Antony, Octavian, and Lepidus. None of them was loyal to Pompey's followers. As had been the case with the First Triumvirate, it was equally true that none was loyal to the others, either. Although three of Caesar's Populares followers held firm control over the Optimates, they had no control over each other.

The Second Triumvirate

Yet again, as had been the case so many times before, the Senate found itself yielding to a rebel with a threatening Roman army. This time, it was a nineteen-year-old. Cicero's strategy of trying to align Octavian against Antony had failed, mainly because the most powerful leaders of the Optimates, Cassius and Brutus, lacked the strength to oppose Octavian, Lepidus, and Antony, and because, as the leaders of the assassins, they were detested by many Romans, especially Octavian.

Now, at the age of twenty, Octavian had amazed Rome by firmly commanding several legions and controlling many respected politicians. However, he realized that he could not continue to defy Cicero and the Optimates by himself forever. He had also learned about history. He knew that the allegiance of Roman legions could be bought with promises of land and money. Octavian was not so naive to think that he alone had loyal legions. He knew that Antony was busy gathering troops, as was Lepidus. Rather than confront the Optimates opposition as well as Antony and Lepidus, Octavian followed Caesar's example and created a triumvirate.

In November 43 B.C., Octavian met with Lepidus and Antony on a small, remote island. All the men

Source Document

In my nineteenth year, on my own initiative and at my own expense, I raised an army with which I set free the state, which was oppressed by the domination of a faction. For that reason, the senate enrolled me in its order by laudatory resolutions . . . assigning me the place of a consul in the giving of opinions, and gave me the imperium. . . . [I]t ordered me, together with the consuls, to take care lest any detriment befall the state. But the people made me consul in the same year, when the consuls each perished in battle, and they made me a triumvir for the settling of the state.[2]

Octavian later wrote this account of his own rise to power.

brought their legions with them as a show of strength. After a brief meeting to reconcile their differences, they divided up the provinces among themselves. They also decided to let Lepidus be consul for 42 B.C., while Octavian and Antony would attack the Optimates armies in Greece led by Caesar's assassins, Cassius and Brutus. This treaty, unlike the private First Triumvirate, became a piece of public legislation. In effect, the three members of the Second Triumvirate replaced the dictatorship of Caesar with the dictatorship of Octavian, Antony, and Lepidus. To advertise their alliance to all of Rome, the three men had coins struck bearing their portraits.

This done, and in possession of a combined forty-five legions, the triumvirs sought money and the elimination of their political rivals. Here, they broke from Caesar's program of extending forgiveness to enemies. Instead, they carried out a campaign of ruthless murder and confiscation of money and property. By the time they were done with their political enemies, some three hundred senators and more than two thousand other influential politicians were killed and dumped into the Tiber River.

The most famous Pompey loyalist caught in this net of ruthless murder was the great orator and politician, Cicero. Antony personally signed the death warrant because of verbal attacks Cicero had made against him earlier. Troops sent to kill Cicero caught him as he attempted to flee on a boat. Sixty-three years old, and seeing no avenue of escape, Cicero told his slaves to run for their lives as he met death with remarkable courage at the point of a sword. To punctuate the hatred Antony felt toward Cicero, he ordered Cicero's head and hands cut off, carried back to Rome, and nailed to the Rostrum in the Forum.

Thus ended the life of one of the most remarkable men in Roman history. Born in relative obscurity, far from the aristocratic trappings of the likes of Caesar and Pompey, Cicero was a *novus homo*, a new man, and a self-made man from a rural town. Believing in the worth of the Republic, Cicero sought to create a peace that would avert the destructive collision of men who placed their ambitions above the good of the general public. Cicero was not without fault, but he tried to steer history along a path that he believed would best suit the Republic.

Death to Caesar's Assassins

Having eliminated all opposition in Rome, the triumvirate now turned its attention to Greece. There, Cassius and Brutus had raised an army eighty thousand strong. Remembering how adeptly Antony had turned the mob in the Forum against them during Caesar's funeral, the assassins realized that they had grossly misread public opinion when they thought that all of Rome would hail them as heroes for killing Caesar. These two assassins fled to Greece. They hoped to find a safe haven where they could raise money and troops for another attempt at returning Rome to the old Republican government they had supported under Pompey.

The triumvirate found it could now focus on a common enemy rather than on each other. Leaving Lepidus behind to guard Italy, Octavian and Antony departed for northern Greece with twenty-eight legions to destroy Cassius and Brutus. After a few days of marching, Octavian and Antony found their foes well-entrenched at the city of Philippi.

Octavian and Antony wasted no time attacking Caesar's two assassins. Cassius, whose troops were quickly routed, committed suicide rather than fall into the hands of his mortal enemies. Brutus fled with the remainder of his army.

Three weeks later, Octavian and Antony caught up with Brutus and decisively defeated his army. Like Cassius, rather than surrender to his enemies, Brutus took his own life. Although a few of his legions fled, this last battle effectively ended all Optimates opposition to the triumvirate.

The Second Triumvirate Crumbles

Success against Cassius and Brutus was no guarantee of success for the triumvirate, however. When Octavian and Antony triumphantly returned to Rome, they met with Lepidus to carve up the Roman provinces once again. The decision was made to give Lepidus Africa, while Antony took all the eastern provinces of Greece, Egypt, and Asia Minor. Octavian acquired the western provinces of Spain and Sardinia. Italy, the heartland of the empire, would be ruled jointly by the three men. To seal their alliance, Octavian and Antony followed the example set by Caesar and Pompey many years earlier. They arranged a marriage between Antony and Octavian's sister, Octavia.

Lepidus soon realized that he had received less than his two fellow triumvirs. Although he had received the African provinces, there were no major cities, and although the land was rich in agriculture, it was not as wealthy or exciting as what Antony and

Octavian had each taken. To make matters worse, although Italy was to be jointly ruled by the three, it quickly became clear that Octavian had a firm grip on it, and was adding part of Gaul as well.

Lepidus, feeling foolish for having accepted so little, decided to get even. With twenty-two legions under his command, Lepidus laid claim to the island of Sicily in direct defiance of Octavian. By provoking Octavian, who had proven himself to be a superior general and politician, Lepidus showed his lack of political savvy. Octavian moved against him, knowing that Lepidus's troops were in no mood for more fighting. As Octavian's army approached, Lepidus's army mutinied, leaving Lepidus to beg for mercy at Octavian's feet. Although Lepidus was thrown out of the triumvirate and stripped of all military authority, Octavian spared his life.

With Lepidus out of the way, the friction between Antony and Octavian became more sharply focused. Octavian had helped himself to all the land that had once belonged to Lepidus. The Roman world was now divided between the east and the west.

Cleopatra—Rome's Humiliation

If events involving Lepidus in Sicily had caused a stress fracture in the triumvirate, then events in Egypt with Antony were causing a major break. The issue was actually the queen of Egypt, Cleopatra. This queen was not a newcomer to Roman politics, nor was she a lightweight. Julius Caesar had fallen under her sway following the defeat of Pompey. Although Caesar supported her in a civil war and she bore him a son, he did not allow her to manipulate him or Rome's foreign policy. Antony was not as strong as Caesar.

Following the renewal of the triumvirate, Antony left his new wife, Octavia, Caesar's sister, in Rome and went to Egypt. In defiance of Roman morality and as a direct insult to Octavian, Antony began a love affair with Cleopatra. In 37 B.C., Cleopatra joined Antony on a full-time basis. They lived together as though they were husband and wife. The historical record is a bit obscure at this point as to whether they married, but Antony did acknowledge that he was the father of two of Cleopatra's children—a son named Alexander Helios and a daughter named Cleopatra Selene.

The longer Antony remained in Egypt, the more dependent he became on Cleopatra's money and influence. His relationship with Cleopatra was creating a scandal in Rome and was driving the wedge between Antony and Octavian ever deeper. More and more, Antony was rejecting Roman culture in favor of Egyptian culture. This fact infuriated all of Rome, but especially Octavian and Octavia.

In 33 B.C., what was left of the Second Triumvirate came to an end. Octavian began to attack Antony verbally as a man who was at the mercy of the queen of Egypt. Octavian's attacks on Antony gradually became more frequent and more vicious. When Antony divorced Octavia, the last buffer that had kept the two men from destroying each other dissolved.

Fearing the worst, most of the western provinces swore allegiance to Octavian as the clouds of civil war once again began to swirl. The events leading up to this next civil war were remarkably similar to those of the previous civil war, fifteen years earlier.

Coming of the Second Civil War

As hostilities between Octavian and Antony began to spill over onto the streets of Rome, the citizens must have felt like they were reliving the past. As these two men built up their armies after several years of open animosity, it seemed as though Rome were about to experience a repeat of the Battle of Pharsalus—and indeed, it was.

As Caesar and Pompey had done, two very powerful men with an unquenchably selfish desire for prestige and unassailable dominance were now assembling their armies in Greece. They intended to fight a decisive battle for absolute control of Rome. None of these activities was motivated by a commitment to social reform in Rome. Neither Antony nor Octavian was championing the cause of the urban poor, the downtrodden soldiers, or the impoverished small farmers.

Just as in the civil war between Caesar and Pompey, Greece would be the stage for the coming struggle. In 31 B.C., Antony and Cleopatra crossed from Alexandria, Egypt, to Greece with all his forces and all her money and warships. Upon Antony's arrival, many senators who mistrusted Octavian—largely the same Optimates who had earlier mistrusted his uncle, Caesar—fled to Greece to support him. Antony had hoped to draw Octavian from his western base of support and win a decisive battle in Greece. In terms of military strength, both sides were evenly balanced. Each had about thirty legions and five hundred warships.

When the two armies first met at Actium on the west coast of central Greece, Antony failed to dislodge Octavian's troops from just north of Actium. Realizing that no success would come from further land operations, Antony took to his ships at Cleopatra's recommendation. Marcus Agrippa, Octavian's seasoned admiral, was ready and eager to set sail for the battle against the Egyptian fleet.

Octavian had a better navy and a superior commander in Marcus Agrippa, but Cleopatra had assured Antony that the Egyptian Navy would save the day. However confident she may have been, Agrippa's smaller, faster ships outmaneuvered Antony's huge but undermanned Egyptian galleys. Seeing that a decisive defeat was close at hand, Cleopatra fled back to Egypt with her treasure chest. Antony quickly followed with forty ships. Seeing their leaders in flight, the rest of the Egyptian Navy immediately surrendered. The legions surrendered a few days later.

In 30 B.C., Octavian set sail for Egypt in pursuit of Antony and Cleopatra. Upon his arrival, he occupied the city of Alexandria. Antony's troops, fearing Octavian's dominance, deserted. Antony was left without an army. Hearing a false rumor that Cleopatra had committed suicide, Antony did the same. Octavian then placed Cleopatra under arrest. Preferring to die than to live as Octavian's prisoner, she ordered a venomous snake smuggled to her and committed suicide with its deadly bite.

The End of the Republic

At thirty-one years old, Octavian was now in control of all the Roman legions, the entire treasury, and all the provinces of the Roman Empire. Like Caesar before him, Octavian was thrust to the fore of the most powerful nation in Europe at an exceptionally young age.

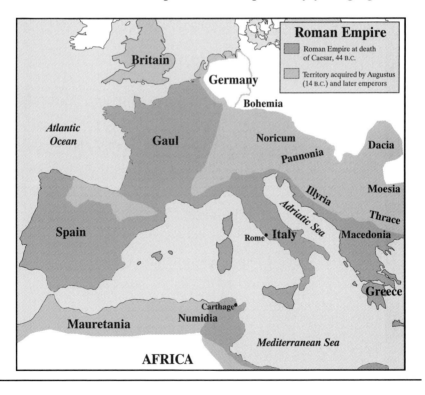

The Roman Empire continued to expand greatly in the years after Julius Caesar's death.

This young man now faced a dilemma. Could he impose the period of peace and prosperity so urgently needed by Rome or was yet another civil war in the making?

None of Octavian's predecessors had provided him with a good example for determining what to do. If he followed Sulla's example of murdering all opposition and then retiring, a fourth civil war would be almost certain. If he followed Caesar's example of arrogantly establishing an absolute dictatorship for life, the old guard Optimates in the Senate would surely build another conspiracy to eliminate him. With history as his teacher, Octavian set about proposing something entirely different.

Now that he had taken absolute control over the Roman Army and faced no serious political opposition, Octavian first paid off his legions for their loyalty in battle. Then he reduced their number from sixty to twenty-eight. To reward them, he paid huge sums of money and gave them land to farm by creating many overseas colonies. Having appeased his legions, Octavian now turned his attention to the citizens of Rome, who had suffered terribly during the last fifty years of civil war.

His first acts were aimed at calming the anxiety of the public by creating an atmosphere of normalcy and tranquillity. He began by forgiving some debt, reducing interest rates, distributing free food, providing lavish public displays of gladiatorial games, and starting building programs throughout Rome. Everywhere citizens went, they found architectural symbols of peace and prosperity.

Octavian next turned his attention to the Senate. He returned to the Senate and the aristocracy their respectability—but not their authority. Like Caesar, he did not carry out a campaign to punish those who had fought against him, and he revoked all unjust orders against them. He also agreed to allow them to pass legislation again, but he maintained veto power over their decisions. In this regard, he restored a form of senatorial status, but not the ultimate authority senators had once enjoyed.

Since Octavian was clearly exercising more ruling authority than a consul, it was time for him to carefully choose a title that would not offend the Senate or the people, but would still convey his enormous power. With the murder of his great-uncle Julius Caesar still fresh in his mind, Octavian did not want the Senate to grant him the title of *dictator perpetuus*. To assist in this matter, the Senate met in 27 B.C. and voted to grant Octavian the title of *Augustus*. This meant a dignified and noble person. Roman historian Dio Cassius wrote:

> Octavian had set his heart strongly on being named Romulus [the first king of Rome]. But when he understood that this aroused suspicions that he desired the kingship, he abandoned his efforts to obtain it and adopted the title of Augustus, as signifying something more than human.[3]

From this time forward, Octavian used Augustus as his name. He never again called himself Octavian.

Octavian, who took on the name Augustus, ruled Rome wisely after the death of his uncle, Julius Caesar.

Because he saw the value of continuing to advertise his link with his adopted father Caesar, he assumed the name *Imperator Caesar Augustus*, meaning Commander in Chief Caesar Augustus. At this point, it was clear to all the citizens of Rome that Augustus held complete authority. As if these honors were not enough, Roman historian Suetonius described the final title the Senate conferred upon Augustus: "The Senate agree with the People of Rome in saluting you as Father of Your Country."[4]

Finally, Augustus decided to take the second title *Princeps*, meaning "first citizen." This would be the formal title that Augustus would use to express his position and to distinguish himself from all previous dictators in Roman history. As Dio Cassius observed, "It was from this time that a monarchy, strictly speaking, was established."[5]

The titles of Augustus and Princeps had no constitutional significance, unlike the offices of consul, tribune, dictator, and senator. Nor did these titles provide Octavian with a legal basis for his authority. As modern historian E. T. Salmon asserted, "He was content to rely on his personal prestige rather than on any official position."[6] What these titles conveyed to the citizens of Rome and to potential rivals for power, as historian H. H. Scullard pointed out, was that "he had more prestige, more moral authority, than any other individual in the State. . . ."[7]

E. T. Salmon further concluded that, with his new titles and his firm control over all of Rome, "Octavian was now in a position to impose his will as he saw fit. The day of the Republic is done; the rule of the Caesars begins."[8]

This event marked the transition from the Republic to the Empire. Augustus would continue to rule as the first Roman emperor until his death in A.D. 14. As the emperor who served the longest tenure, Augustus is also recognized as the architect of the Roman Empire and arguably the greatest emperor of all time. Those aristocratic families that had supported the Optimates throughout the civil wars remained loyal to their cause, but as the emperors came and went, one after another, the hope of reinstating the Republic was eventually lost.

Epilogue for the Republic

When Augustus formally replaced the Republic with the Empire in 27 B.C., the change went largely unnoticed. By this time, Romans of all social classes had become accustomed to a regular diet of one dictator after another descending on Rome at the head of personal armies, running roughshod over the citizenry as well as the old traditions of the Republic. Augustus was merely another.

For average Romans, the transition from the Republic to the Empire made no difference at all. Generally speaking, they remained poor, living in seedy conditions, and they continued to die at early ages from hard work, poor diet, and relentless disease. The transition was not even significant to the handful of privileged aristocrats who had hoped to regain some semblance of their former Republican authority and prestige. Part of Augustus's genius was his ability to return to the Senate and the aristocracy a sense of dignity and purpose without returning to them their former authority. All things considered, little had changed.

Romans at this time did share at least one thing in common: the need to return to peace and prosperity. They cared less about how it was achieved than the fact that someone had finally managed to achieve it. After more than one hundred years of civil strife, everyone could at last look forward to much-needed rest and repair. If there was one thing that Augustus achieved that truly changed the lives of all Romans, it was peace. His forty-one-year reign as the first emperor of Rome earned the name *Pax Romana*, Latin for the period of "Roman Peace."

Caesar's Legacy

Modern Roman historians debate whether the fall of the Republic was inevitable and what role Julius Caesar played in its demise. Most historians believe that evidence for the unavoidable fall of the Republic can be found in the events surrounding the attempted reforms of the Gracchi brothers and the rise of Marius and his private army. As for the second issue, Caesar's role in the demise of the Republic, historians are almost unanimous in their view that he was the central figure. Modern historian H. H. Scullard summarized Caesar's qualities, both good and bad:

Caesar's outstanding abilities are unquestioned. One of the world's greatest soldiers, he was also a writer of great distinction and an orator of the first rank. Urbane, cultured and courteous, he possessed a will of steel and an intensity of intellect that may have been reflected in his tall spare figure, his clear complexion and his lively dark eyes. An aristocrat by birth and nature, he had a true Roman sense of the practical: clear in purpose and swift in decision, he could be ruthless and coldblooded, but was more often clement and generous. The charm, as well as the force, of his personality captivated the loyalty of his troops and supporters, but awareness of his genius engendered in him a certain aloofness.[9]

Of all of the brilliant and significant leaders of the late Republic, Caesar's legacy, more than any other, continued to find expression in the Empire and beyond. During the Empire, the name *Caesar* became a title for the emperors, who were collectively called "The Caesars." Suetonius, the first-century A.D. biographer of Julius Caesar as well as the biographer of the first eleven emperors of the Roman Empire, entitled his book, *The Twelve Caesars*. Many political hopefuls wishing to gain status by associating themselves with Caesar's family often added Caesar as a middle name, even though they had no family connection. Towns named after Caesar sprang up across the Empire.

Many centuries after Rome ceased to be a dominant force in European politics, the Germans borrowed Caesar's name for their supreme ruler. They altered it only slightly to *Kaiser*. The Russians did the same, calling

Julius Caesar is still remembered as one of the most powerful leaders of all time.

their leader *Czar*. One of the greatest tributes to the memory of Julius Caesar comes from the greatest of all English writers, William Shakespeare, who honored Caesar's reputation by writing the play *Julius Caesar*.

To this day, Caesar remains more familiar to modern people worldwide than any other Roman leader. In part, Hollywood movies are responsible for this fact, yet Hollywood reflects the historical record. Even to the ancient historians, Caesar's was the name most revered. Caesar survives today in many arenas. His writings describing his military tactics are read and studied at military academies. Caesar was a brilliant psychologist and manager of troops; business schools today use his writings to teach managers how to lead and encourage their staffs.

Probably the greatest benefit that modern history derives from Caesar's accomplishments is the interest his name still generates. Travelers and students visiting Rome and other ancient historical sites continue to search out the places where Caesar walked, conducted war, and made history. Few names of great leaders from the distant past continue to attract the attention his does. As long as the name Caesar is recognized, Roman history will continue to be alive and be studied as one of the great periods of Western civilization.

Timeline

Dates are B.C.

753—Period of the Roman kings.
–509

509—Republic begins.

264—The Punic Wars are waged; Rome rises as the
–146 dominant Mediterranean power.

133—Tiberius Gracchus, the first of the Populares,
–132 proposes reforms that would provide land and
assistance to landless peasants; He and three
hundred supporters are killed by a group of senators
and their clients.

123—Gaius Sempronius Gracchus, younger brother of
–111 Tiberius, proposes even more radical and extensive
reforms; He is killed along with three thousand
supporters.

107—Marius successfully raises a private army to conduct
–101 a war against Jugurtha.

100—Caesar is born.

82—Civil war between Marius and Sulla.

82—Sulla's dictatorship.
–79

73—Spartacus's slave revolt.
–71

60—First Triumvirate of Caesar, Crassus, and Pompey is
formed.

49—Caesar crosses the Rubicon River, initiating a
second civil war.

49—Civil war between Caesar and Pompey.
–45

44—Caesar's assassination by Cassius, Brutus, and their fellow conspirators.

43—Second Triumvirate of Octavian, Marc Antony, and Lepidus is formed.

42—Antony and Octavian defeat Cassius and Brutus.

31—Civil war between Octavian and Antony.

27—Octavian is named Augustus, first emperor of the Roman Empire.

27—The period of the Roman Empire.
–A.D. 476

Chapter Notes

Chapter 1. The Die Is Cast

1. Erich Gruen, *The Last Generation of the Roman Republic* (Berkeley: University of California Press, 1974), p. 1.

Chapter 2. Rome at the Crossroads

1. John Porter, trans., *Polybius 6.11–18: The Constitution of the Roman Republic*, September 22, 1999, <http://www.usask.ca/antarch/cnea/DeptTransls/Polybius .html> (December 6, 2000).

2. Paul Halsall, "Ancient History Sourcebook: Polybius (c. 200–after 118 BCE): Rome at the End of the Punic Wars," *Ancient History Sourcebook*, May 1998, <http://www.fordham.edu/halsall/ancient/polybius6.html> (December 6, 2000).

3. Polybius, *The Histories of Polybius*, trans. W. R. Patton (Cambridge, Mass.: Harvard University Press, 1960), vol. 1, pp. 3, 5.

Chapter 3. Civil Strife and the Late Republic

1. H. H. Scullard, *From the Gracchi to Nero: A History of Rome from 133 B.C. to A.D. 68* (London: Methuen & Co. Ltd., 1963), p. 18.

2. Paul Halsall, "Ancient History Sourcebook: Appian: The Civil Wars—On the Gracchi," *Ancient History Sourcebook*, May 1998, <http://www.fordham.edu/halsall/ ancient/appian-civwars1.html> (December 6, 2000).

Chapter 4. The Rome of Young Caesar

1. Suetonius, *The Twelve Caesars*, trans. Robert Graves (London: Penguin Books, 1979), p. 34.

2. Plutarch, *Fall of the Roman Republic, Six Lives by Plutarch, Life of Sulla*, trans. Rex Warner (London: Penguin Books, 1958), pp. 104–105.

3. Erich Gruen, *The Last Generation of the Roman Republic* (Berkeley: University of California Press, 1974), pp. 9–10.

4. Ibid., p. 445.

Chapter 5. Caesar's Rise to Power

1. Plutarch, "Caesar," *Internet Classics Archive,* 1994–2000, <http://classics.mit.edu/Plutarch/caesar.html> (December 6, 2000).

2. Plutarch, *Fall of the Roman Republic, Six Lives by Plutarch, Life of Caesar*, trans. Rex Warner (London: Penguin Books, 1958), p. 255.

3. Plutarch, *Fall of the Roman Republic, Six Lives by Plutarch, Life of Crassus,* trans. Rex Warner (London: Penguin Books, 1958), p. 127.

4. H. H. Scullard, *From the Gracchi to Nero: A History of Rome from 133 B.C. to A.D. 68* (London: Methuen & Co. Ltd., 1963), p. 115.

5. Suetonius, *The Twelve Caesars*, trans. Robert Graves (London: Penguin Books, 1979), p. 40.

6. Bruce J. Butterfield, "De bello gallico (Gallic Wars): Book 1," *Julius Caesar's War Commentaries*, 1996, <http://mcadams.posc.mu.edu/txt/caesar/CAEGAL01.HTM> (December 6, 2000).

Chapter 6. A Clash of Titans—Caesar Versus Pompey

1. Erich Gruen, *The Last Generation of the Roman Republic* (Berkeley: University of California Press, 1974), p. 384.

2. Matthias Gelzer, *Caesar Politician and Statesman,* trans. Peter Needham (Oxford: Basil Blackwell, 1968), p. 195.

3. Ibid., p. 210.

4. Suetonius, *The Twelve Caesars*, trans. Robert Graves (London: Penguin Books, 1979), pp. 28–29.

5. Gelzer, p. 194.

6. William McDermott, *Lectures on the Late Republic*, University of Pennsylvania, 1970.

7. H. H. Scullard, *From the Gracchi to Nero: A History of Rome from 133 B.C. to A.D. 68* (London: Methuen & Co. Ltd., 1963), p. 154.

8. Marcus Tullius Cicero, "A Dictator Comes to Dinner, Rome, 45 BC," *The Mammoth Book of Eyewitness History*, ed. Jon E. Lewis (New York: Carroll & Graf Publishers, Inc., 1998), p. 23.

9. Gelzer, p. 325.

10. Suetonius, pp. 50–51.

11. Plutarch, *Makers of Rome*, trans. Ian Scott-Kilvert (London: Penguin Books, 1965), p. 283.

Chapter 7. The Final Agony—Octavian Versus Antony

1. H. H. Scullard, *From the Gracchi to Nero: A History of Rome from 133 B.C. to A.D. 68* (London: Methuen & Co. Ltd., 1963), p. 156.

2. Thomas Bushnell, "The Deeds of Divine Augustus," *The Internet Classics Archive*, 1994–2000, <http://classics.mit.edu/Augustus/deeds.html> (December 6, 2000).

3. Dio Cassius, *Roman History*, trans. Ian Scott-Kilvert (New York: Penguin Books, 1987), p. 140.

4. Suetonius, *The Twelve Caesars*, trans. Robert Graves (London: Penguin Books, 1979), p. 87.

5. Cassius, p. 140.

6. Edward T. Salmon, *A History of the Roman World from 30 B.C. to A.D. 138* (London: Methuen & Co. Ltd., 1966), p. 10.

7. Scullard, p. 219.

8. Salmon, p. 1.

9. Scullard, p. 158.

Further Reading

Bernard, Charlotte. *Caesar & Rome*. Brookfield, Conn.: Twenty-First Century Books, 1995.

Cassius, Dio. *Roman History*, trans. Ian Scott-Kilvert. New York: Penguin Books, 1987.

Green, Robert. *Julius Caesar*. Danbury, Conn.: Franklin Watts, 1996.

Nardo, Don. *Caesar's Conquest of Gaul*. San Diego, Calif.: Lucent Books, 1996.

———. *Julius Caesar*. San Diego, Calif.: Lucent Books, 1997.

Suetonius. *The Twelve Caesars*, trans. Robert Graves. London: Penguin Books, 1979.

Internet Addresses

Butterfield, Bruce J. *Julius Caesar's War Commentaries.* 1996. <http://mcadams.posc.mu.edu/txt/caesar/index.htm>.

Halsall, Paul. *Ancient History Sourcebook.* May 1998. <http://www.fordham.edu/halsall/ancient/asbook.html>.

"Julius Caesar." *The Rulers of the Roman World.* n.d. <http://myron.sjsu.edu/romeweb/EMPCONT/empcont.htm>.

Plutarch. "Caesar." *Internet Classics Archive.* 1994–2000. <http://classics.mit.edu/Plutarch/caesar.html>.

Index